RAISING BOYS' ACHIEVEMENT IN SCHOOLS

RAISING BOYS' ACHIEVEMENT IN SCHOOLS

Edited by Kevan Bleach

Trentham Books

First published in 1998 by Trentham Books Limited

Trentham Books Limited
Westview House
734 London Road
Oakhill
Stoke on Trent
Staffordshire
England ST4 5NP

British Cataloguing in Publication Data
A catalogue record for this book is available from the British Library
ISBN 1 85856 103 5
(hb ISBN 1 85856 142 6)

Designed and typeset by Trentham Print Design Ltd., Chester and
printed in Great Britain by Redwood Books, Wiltshire

Contents

Acknowledgements

As editor, I wish to thank all my contributors. All are practising teachers, senior managers, advisers, lecturers or consultants who have experienced as many pressures on their time and energy as I have. Nevertheless, everybody willingly and generously agreed to contribute to this project when first I discussed it with Professor John Eggleston of Warwick University.

I am grateful, and honoured, to include a Foreword from Professor Tim Brighouse, who is Chief Education Officer for Birmingham. He has a long, varied and distinguished career in education. In the few years he has been at Birmingham, the qualities and values that inform his visionary leadership have had a profoundly uplifting effect on the city's education service.

On a personal note, I owe so much to my wife Susan for the forbearance she has shown during the months that I have spent writing and editing this book.

Foreword

When teachers start to analyse their practice and observe closely the effects of their teaching either as individuals or as groups on the children they teach, exciting things usually start to happen. They fire each other with questions: *'Why is it that boys each year in our school score much lower on points per pupil at GCSE and in Key Stage 3 results than they do in the Abbey School on the other side of town?'* *'Yes, but not in History – why is that? Is George doing something we are not?'* *'How about their attendance patterns?'* *'And why do some of our tutors have so much better attendance and Key Stage 3 results although they have more mixed ability groups than others? Has anyone looked at the tutors' impact?'*

Once the questions start they are hard to stop. Indeed, who would want to stop them? For a school where staff ask questions, quote evidence, plan together, observe each other's practice, and talk about teaching and learning, is a good school. It is, in effect, a research and learning community.

All that starts with some practitioners identifying a problem and being determined to do something about it. This book illustrates both some case studies of schools who have done precisely that, but also a topic which baffles us all. What do we do about boys' under-achievement?

I walked round a primary school in Birmingham where the boys' performance was as good as the girls'. The Head and I were talking about it. The Head was a man and he was always talking to the children. We walked about the school and his conversation in the corridors and the playground was always punctuated by questions to the boys about sport and pastimes out of school. We speculated together about the possibility that such conversations may be affecting the self-esteem and, therefore, the performance of the pupils. He agreed, though he had never thought about it before, that his conversation with pupils was always about sport and boy-inclined interests. We wondered together if that had an effect – or if the absence of it would? Not a total effect, of course, but a contributory effect.

Well, of course, that's anecdotal. But this book is not. It addresses one of the most important issues of our time and it does so compellingly. It will help those who want to find solutions, not problems, to get closer to their goals. As such, it deserves a wide readership.

Tim Brighouse

Notes on contributors

Kevan Bleach is Senior Teacher at Sneyd Community School, Walsall, and Visiting Lecturer at Wolverhampton University School of Education. He has worked on different aspects of gender, education and management, contributing extensively to INSET courses. He is currently researching for his EdD at Lincoln University.

Wendy Bradford is Acting Headteacher at King James' School, Almondbury, Huddersfield. She is the author of *Raising Boys' Achievement,* published by Kirklees LEA. She is currently researching for her PhD at Huddersfield University.

Alan Davison is Headteacher of Mill Hill County High School, Barnet. He was formerly Head at Notley High School, Braintree, Essex.

Chris Edwards is Deputy Head at Notley. They led a project, funded by Essex County Council, designed to boost boys' achievement by offering them a change in their styles of learning.

Graham Frater is an education consultant and former English specialist with HMI. He has just completed a major project on improving boys' literacy on behalf of the Basic Skills Agency.

Brian Matthews is a Lecturer in Science Education at Goldsmiths College, University of London. He has been engaged in research into ways of enabling boys and girls to communicate while learning together.

Colin Noble is an Adviser with Kirklees LEA School Effectiveness Service. He currently manages its *Raising Boys' Achievement* project and was a contributor to the video and case studies in the authority's resource pack.

Val Penny is Senior Teacher at Orleton Park School, Telford, and was formerly Head of English at Wakeman School, Shrewsbury. She was a member of the Shropshire RAISE Boys and English project. Also, she has been involved in several other projects supported by SCAA and the Centre for the Study of Comprehensive Schools.

John Ryder is Deputy Head at The Boswells School, Chelmsford, Essex. There, he has worked with senior colleagues on various strategies for encouraging boys to work harder.

Beverley Swan is Head of Lower School at Shenfield High School, Brentwood, Essex. She is currently pursuing an MA in Education, with boys' underachievement as her main research theme.

Brian Terry is an education consultant who leads courses and contributes to the national debate on raising boys' achievement. He was formerly an Area TVEI Co-ordinator for Humberside. **Liz Terry** is Headteacher of Pool Community School, Redruth, Cornwall, and was formerly Head of the Vale of Ancholme School, North Lincolnshire.

Introduction

Harry Enfield recently confessed about *his* days as an 'under-achieving' schoolboy. He had a good O-level History teacher whose passion for relating battles and mutinies made him occasionally lose control of his bodily functions. He would get so carried away that his outbursts of wind caused Harry and his friends to weep with giggles. They entered History lessons eagerly anticipating not the causes of the Indian Mutiny, but their teacher's trumpeting trousers! Their conduct as sixth formers was no less immature. Economics lessons, for instance, were spent drawing genitalia on pictures of Jim Callaghan and President Carter in *The Economist*. Harry Enfield's point was that modern teenage boys are no stupider than in his schooldays. What has altered is that they are now wrongly assumed to have the maturity of their female peers. He was more concerned about boys' *attainment*, however. Twenty years ago, they did better than girls, but now...? Is it the school system, he asked, that is letting them down?

In one sense, Enfield is perfectly right. It has long been accepted that boys mature later in adolescence. While they were inclined to be idle and mess about through their pre-16 education, girls were conspicuously industrious, although the boys tended to catch up by the time of O-levels. So perhaps the phenomenon of 'new laddism' is just the old-fashioned problem of boys behaving badly (Chaudhary, 1998, 6). However, as we are well aware from the battery of published test and examination results, reinforced by press articles and the statements of government ministers, there are now clearly significant differences in the achievements of boys and girls. Indeed, the worrying performance of boys extends beyond public examinations like SATs and GCSEs to literacy, university admissions, special needs provision, truancy and crime (McDonagh, 1998, 16).

Here are just a few findings about various forms of under-achievement by boys that appeared in the press in the days following Stephen Byers' address on the subject at the International Congress on School Effectiveness and Improvement in Manchester last January:

- Test results for 1997 show a similar gender gap to that in 1996, when 7-year-old boys were 9 per cent behind girls for reading and 10 per cent for English, rising to a 15 per cent gap for 11-year-olds and 18 per cent at 14 (*Daily Telegraph*, 5/1/98).

- Last year, more girls achieved five good GCSE passes at grade C or above in every education authority in England, except Kensington and Chelsea (*Wolverhampton Express & Star*, 5/1/98).

- 28,500 boys leave school each year with no qualifications, compared with 21,500 girls (*The Guardian,* 5/1/98).

- Boys make up 83 per cent of pupils who are permanently excluded from school in England and Wales (*TES*, 9/1/98).

- Scotland Yard has warned that children aged between 14 and 16 are responsible for 40 per cent of London street crime. The majority are male, many of them illiterate (*Daily Telegraph*, 5/1/98).

What has demonstrated most significantly the disparity in performance between boys and girls is the publication, year after year, of GCSE results. Girls started to move ahead with the introduction of the new GCSE courses in 1988. In 1987, the final year of O-level and CSE, the difference in favour of girls gaining five or more A-C grades was a mere 1.6 per cent. By 1990, it had increased to 7.6 per cent and by 1995 to 9.1 per cent (SCAA, 1996, 8-9). But in the flurry of grades and percentages and troubled newspaper headlines, one important point has been overlooked. Girls have *not* improved their grades at the expense of boys. The overall success of both genders has been improving since GCSE started, so boys' achievement is not worsening in absolute terms. What is happening is that girls are outpacing boys and to an increasing degree, although significant differences exist between schools and between subjects within schools (SCAA, *ibid*; NEAB, 1996, 6-7; Pickering, 1997, 33).

However, certain groups of boys *are* doing particularly badly. Chris Woodhead, HM Chief Inspector of Schools, has drawn attention to the plight of white, working-class boys who find themselves caught in a vicious circle of under-achievement at school (1996, 18). Figures show many African Caribbean boys to be in a similar position. Some would say it is social class and cultural factors, rather than gender, which have the single most important impact on educational attainment in British schools. To what extent, for instance, is the weak performance of working-class girls being hidden by the sterling achievements of middle-class girls (Plummer, 1998, 21)? One would not expect to find significant gender differences amongst the children of the most affluent families. Yet the phenomenon of male under-achievement has been noted recently among boys who attend independent schools (Power *et al.*, 1997).

The case for a more nuanced response to differences in boys' and girls' performances is supported by the fact that girls lose the edge over boys in the top grades at A-level. Of course, the low-achievers have dropped out by this stage, but another factor is probably the style of examination and assessment at post-16. The flair and confidence and risk-taking demonstrated by some boys is more advantageous than the sustained work and good organisation used to such good effect by many girls at GCSE (Elwood, 1996). A similar explanation may well apply to the fact that more men than women get firsts and 2.1 honours degrees at Oxbridge and elsewhere (MacLeod, 1997).

We should be wary, therefore, of portraying 'boys' as an homogeneous group of under-achievers who are all 'victims' of the education system in terms of pedagogy and practice. Nonetheless, the publication of examination results *has* stimulated a tremendous interest in gender differences that extends well beyond the confines of the teaching profession. A generation ago, the under-achievement of girls was identified as a national concern and teachers and educationalists responded very positively to the need to improve their opportunities at school. Now, commentators are suggesting that 'the future is female' and voicing concern about our 'lost boys'. The challenge has been reversed. Indeed, there has never been greater public interest in the effects of gender on educational achievement, judging by the number of research projects, press articles, television programmes and radio 'phone-ins.

The immediate concern for schools is what practical strategies can be set in motion for improving boys' performance. That is where the nature and focus of this book becomes relevant. Since involving myself a couple of years ago in a practitioner research project investigating factors influencing the motivation and performance of Year 8 boys in a typical urban comprehensive, I have become aware of the wealth of interesting work taking place at school, LEA and university research levels. This upsurge of concern and activity is a welcome move and offers reassurance to teachers in individual schools that they are not on their own. There is a general purpose and direction to all the work that is taking place. So when Professor John Eggleston, of Warwick University, contacted me, after reading in the *Times Educational Supplement* about my school-based project, to suggest writing a book, I responded with the idea of a series of case studies that would highlight the range of strategies and good practice currently being developed.

The contributors I have brought together in this book are all school-based researcher-practitioners who have developed experience and expertise in various aspects of the boys and achievement issue. Their case studies are intended to provide teachers and managers with a rich menu of practical ideas, insights and measures from which to choose when dealing with this vital area. I think they would all agree with me that there are no 'quick fixes' in their chapters. Each of us deals with just the tip of an iceberg – and that iceberg is the product of boys' experiences and expectations of subjects in schools, discrepancies with girls in their language skills deriving from their infant days, traditional styles of child rearing and socialisation, *and* the new uncertainty surrounding the role of the male in our changing society.

The task ahead of us certainly looks daunting! Nevertheless, teachers committed to boosting the standards of boys' performance will benefit from raising each other's awareness of the issues and in sharing ideas about possible ways forward. We should never lose sight of the observation made by OFSTED that the most crucial factor in improving boys' attitudes and performance in English is *the influence of the teacher.* And in seeking to improve the quality of the teaching and learning and schooling experiences provided for boys along any of the different lines suggested in the following chapters, we shall be raising the expectations and standards for *both* genders, thus creating an ethos of success and excellence for *all* pupils. It is a challenge and an opportunity we should welcome with enthusiasm.

References

Chaudhary V (1998): Problems that arise when boys will be lads. *The Guardian.* 6/1/98, 6.

Elwood J and Comber C (1996): Results: a question of perceptions, not gender. *The Independent.* 15/8/96.

MacLeod D (1997): The Oxbridge problem. *The Guardian Higher Education.* 17/6/97, i.

McDonagh M (1998): Time we had jobs for the boys. *Daily Telegraph,* 5/1/98, 16.

NEAB (1996): Gender differences in the GCSE. *NEAB Standard.* Summer 1996, 6-7.

Pickering J (1997): *Raising Boys' Achievement.* Stafford, Network Educational Press.

Plummer G (1998): Forget gender, class is still the real divide. *Times Educational Supplement.* 23/1/98, 21.

Power S, Edwards T, Whitty G and Wigfall V (1997): *Schoolboys and schoolwork: gender identification and academic achievement.* Bristol, University of Bristol.

SCAA (1996): *GCSE Results Analysis.* London, SCAA.

Woodhead C (1996): Boys who learn to be losers. *The Times.* 6/3/96, 18.

1

Why the likely lads lag behind
an examination of reasons for some boys' poor academic performance and behaviour in school

Kevan Bleach

This chapter is a generalised summary of research findings and opinions about the likely factors influencing boys' motivation and performance at school. What becomes rapidly obvious is that there are many commonly-held explanations about the under-achievement of boys. They range from genetic and physiological factors, to the socialisation and expectations boys face at home, to the possibly superfluous role of males in an increasingly globalised, hi-tech, service economy that prefers to employ women. And all this is *before* we think about what is happening in our classrooms! Some of these explanations involve essentially speculative and stereotypical views. Many of them are interlinked. Anyone can think of exceptions and many of the issues touched upon are far more complex than it is possible to demonstrate in this brief overview.

An important caveat concerns the danger of regarding boys as one homogeneous group. Equal opportunities work in the past on gender tended to lump boys together, rather than recognise their plurality. The recent development of a critical research literature on 'masculinity' and schooling, however, suggests that it manifests itself in a *variety* of forms (see, for instance Mac an Ghaill, 1994). As a gender, boys display types of masculinity that can be complex and contradictory and often in conflict with each other in terms of a 'pecking order' of interests. This extends to individuals, in that within each boy one can find multiple masculine identities struggling for dominance (Jackson and Salisbury, 1996, 107-109). Differences in ethnicity, class and sexuality further serve to undermine it as a monolithic concept (see, for instance, Mac an Ghaill, 1988; Sewell, 1997). So in considering the various factors responsible for problematising adolescent masculinity, we must bear in mind its essential diversity.

Blame nature, not nurture?

The first area that merits comment concerns the biological explanations for differences between boys and girls. Although, like all other aspects of this debate, they incite strong disagreements, there appears to be a growing post-feminist belief that males and females are different, after all. In this respect, perhaps the womb is the most fruitful area to begin any investigation. Research on the growing foetus has indicated that females can be observed moving their mouths at an earlier stage, which may reflect a more general pattern of advanced development from conception (Fletcher, 1997, 9). From birth, girls are certainly regarded as more sensitive to sound and the detection of intonation patterns, thereby making them more likely to learn language earlier (Downes, 1994, 5).

Variations in spatial visualisation are traceable to a recessive gene in the X-chromosome, the role of sex hormones and differences in brain lateralisation (Shuard, 1983, cited in Stobart *et al.*, 1992, 266). Boys' possession of an X and a Y chromosome, whereas girls have two Xs, may genetically programme some boys to be less aware of others' feelings, demanding of their time and unintentionally offensive. If scientists who make this claim are right, it may help to explain why girls tend to be better able to size up and cope with situations than their gauche male counterparts. Boys often have to learn social skills – like tact, social deftness and intuition – the hard way (Hawkes, 1997, 5; Utley, 1997, 9).

Neurology includes many studies suggesting close links between the brain and gender. Experiments at Yale, for instance, have put male and female subjects through a battery of psychological tests, during which their brains were scanned for activity by measuring blood flow. These reveal tasks being processed in both halves of the female brain, but predominantly in one half of the male brain, thus suggesting gender differences in how individuals think (Kohn, 1995, 13-16). More recently, a Sydney University neurologist reported finding that areas of the brain associated with language are more highly developed in women, which may further account for females having better aptitudes for language and social skills (Marrin, 1997, 34).

Much of this research is still in its infancy, which makes it appropriate to draw a distinction between the *evidence* for differences and *assertion* about their significance. There should be further caution about reading too much into such evidence for fear of thinking there is nothing that we, as teachers, can do about the aspects of boys' behaviour to which it is related. The dangers of having one's perceptions shaped by a sense of biological determinism – namely, that boys are disadvantaged from the start – are readily seen in excessive newspaper headlines like '*Boys are oafish because they can't help it*' or '*The sensitive sex was born that way*'. A generation ago, Maccoby and Jacklin (1974) offered a systematic analysis of research projects on the psychology of gender differences. They found some to be supported by impressive evidence, others inadequately tested, and still others to be pure myth. It is right that we should remain cautious. However, given the rapid advances in scanning technology, new information on gender differences in brain function – and the implications these have for thinking and behaviour – is likely to continue appearing.

Socialisation and expectation

A more fruitful source of explanation for differences between boys and girls, in terms of scope for school improvement, lies in environmental hypotheses. These include cultural, social and psychological influences that affect boys' learning and performance through various processes: 'different out-of-school experiences, different within-school experiences, perceived male and female domains, differences in attitude, self-image and expectations of success' (Gipps, 1994, 150). There is corroboration in the relative changes in achievement by men and women over the last hundred years, which reflect changing social structures and expectations rather than any transformation in female intellectual ability. Little overall variability in performance exists between the sexes compared with differences between males or between females (Stobart *et al.*, 1992, 266).

Differences first manifest themselves in playgroups and then extend through the early years of primary school, as documented in a recent study by Patricia Murphy, of the Open University, and Jannette Elwood, of the London University Institute of Education:

Playgroup

Boys make straight for the construction toys or the bikes while the girls are playing in the home corner, doing a drawing or talking to an adult. Children have already developed clear ideas of what boys do and girls do. 'Boys are racing all around the garden being somebody else or being the leader. Girls – you find them sitting in a corner playing their quiet games,' were observations from playgroup staff... Each are practising different types of talk, a mother-child discussion as opposed to arresting a baddie, for instance.

Reception

Boys arrive with an interest in information books and are likely to find reading schemes, based largely on stories about people, harder to get into. They may also be at a disadvantage in learning to write because they are less good with pencils... Even when boys and girls are following the same activity, like playing with Lego, they are doing it differently. Boys made vehicles or guns, using moveable parts, while girls made simple houses to use in a social game.

Donald MacLeod: The gender divide. *Guardian Education*. 17/6/97, 3

From seven, boys and girls are already displaying differing attitudes to the demands of school. Girls are more conscientious and concerned about presentation, they listen and pay attention, and they socialise with a considerable amount of mutual accord. They tend to play without supervision, establishing their own rules and roles for each other in a way that mimics adult behaviour. Boys, by contrast, are more noisy and attention-seeking; they find it difficult to sit still and pay attention.

By eleven, girls are progressing in reading and verbal and non-verbal tests (see, for instance, Sammons, 1996, 479).

They start their new secondary school with greater maturity, which is possibly linked to their pre-pubescent state, and are more likely to be working on-task and to set high standards for themselves. Perhaps this was why, when more girls than boys regularly passed the eleven-plus, some local authorities imposed limits on female entry to grammar schools to stop them monopolising the places (Grant, 1996, p 6). The justification for weighting the examination in boys' favour was that girls developed earlier – the boys would catch up with girls when they matured in their teens and over-take them at O-level.

Girls tend to have a compliant motivational style, while boys want to do everything quickly and prefer short-term tasks. They do not take so much care with the standard of their work, they are reluctant to do extra work and they read less. They are less attentive in class, being more concerned with the 'laddish' traits of acting in a lively manner and having a good laugh (Downes, 1994, 5; Warrington and Younger, 1997, 22). Of course, this is *not* true for all boys. However, the identification that *some* of them make with 'macho' values leads them to regard a studious approach as 'unmanly'. Indeed, their resentment and defiance can extend to more disruptive and threatening activities, such as class-room disruption, vandalism and bullying and harassment of girls and other boys. The pressure to conform to this gender stereotype can lead to a 'second rank' of boys seeking to give the impression of not work-ing hard or appearing to enjoy school, while drawing the line at more overt defiance. All of this has worrying implications for teacher time, energies and school resources, as well as the classroom time the boys in question are losing (Jackson and Salisbury, 1996, 104; Pickering, 1997, 38).

More boys are in need of special needs assistance. Primary school boys, for instance, are up to eight times more likely to be identified as having special educational needs than their female classmates, accord-ing to a study of 359 SEN pupils in 28 schools, funded by the Economic and Social Research Council. The boy-girl disparity is parti-cularly pronounced among white pupils in the categories of emotional and behavioural difficulties. Part of the reason for this may be that boys' learning seems to be more teacher dependent than girls' and they are also more inclined to display anti-learning behaviour. By contrast, girls generally support each other's learning and tend to keep out of SEN provision (Budge, 1997). The trend is also obvious from the gender make-up of the special units for pupils excluded from mainstream schools (O'Leary and Charter, 1996).

In early adolescence, girls are more likely to be found in the house, reading and chatting and doing their homework. Boys, on the other hand, grow up with an emphasis on doing, rather than talking. They are more likely to be out playing and engaging in activities involving physical daring. Their central learning style is experiential and they fail to develop the 'feminine' reflective abilities of analysing, discussing and expressing feelings (Hinds, 1995, p 12). In school, they are more likely to participate in open discussions and physical involvement, rather than sitting and writing. Part of the problem is their concentration span: the 'typical' 13-14-year-old boy concentrates for only 4-5 minutes, compared with 13 minutes for girls, thereby underlining the need for more constant interaction with their teachers (Lightfoot, 1997).

The OFSTED report, *Boys and English*, vigorously brought to light boys' poor performance, especially in literacy skills. They have narrower experiences of fiction, write more predictably and have difficulty with the affective aspects of English (OFSTED, 1993). Literature has particular problems, as boys are inclined to see less importance in understanding character, motivation or theme (Hinds, 1995, p 12). A Shropshire LEA survey of reading habits in Year 9 pupils showed a sharp difference between boys and girls. While nearly half the girls said they 'liked reading a lot', less than a fifth of boys did. Only 8 per cent of boys shared books with friends, compared with three-quarters of girls (Klein, 1995, iv). These findings confirm other surveys, over the last 25 years, of children's voluntary reading habits, which have reported the particular decline in boys' reading by the age of 14.

Role models in books with whom they can identify are important for stimulating boys' interest in reading, according to a survey of 8,834 young people carried out by the Children's Literature Research Centre:

He's got to be so macho

[There is a] changing perception of masculinity. The male heroes of early boys' fiction, such as *Tom Brown's Schooldays* (1857) by Thomas Hughes, display emotions, were compassionate, and combined active lives with an ethos of self-sacrifice and service... Reading, however, unless done to acquire information, came increasingly to be seen as the reverse of manly... The 'boys' book soon had a clear set of distinguishing characteristics: they followed the action-packed adventures and conquests of two-dimensional characters in an all-male world... On the whole, uncomplicated, unreflective, anti-intellectual and non-reading males became the fictional role models for a generation of boys. Despite high levels of excitement, 'boys' books failed to provide a satisfying literary diet. Increasingly, boys turned away from fiction.

Kim Reynolds: He's got to be so macho. *Guardian Education*. 8/10/96,

So if non-reading boys are to be encouraged to read more, attention needs to be paid to what will provide them with greater narrative satisfaction. Role models at home are important, too. If boys do not witness their fathers reading and the only people who teach them to read are females in the family and their (largely female) primary school teachers, getting absorbed in a book runs the risk of being perceived as a 'sissy', rather than 'masculine', pursuit. It is a sad fact that in some families, literacy is seen as essentially the mother's work because it draws on skills and abilities in which females show strength (Way, 1997, 12). On the other hand, research suggests that fathers are more likely to help sons, rather than daughters, with ICT and mathematical activities, which echoes the traditional passing-on of male skills with tools and machinery (David and Weiner, 1997, 23).

A survey on language, conducted by the Assessment of Performance Unit (APU), demonstrated how reading interests affect children's styles of writing. Girls' reading tastes are very wide and include a lot of fiction, especially novels dealing with emotions and relationships; by contrast, boys exhibit narrower preferences, choosing non-fiction information books or technical manuals relating to their interests or hobbies that encourage competence in information-sifting and selection. Facts have a high currency – hence the popularity of 'fact files' and 'record breakers'. A new report by the Qualifications and

Curriculum Authority (QCA) claims boys dislike most fiction – apart from sport, fantasy and action stories – and think poetry is written by effete eccentrics (Petre, 1998, 4). Reading performance in school improves where topics are matched to boys' preferences. Book covers attract them, particularly if there is a film or television tie-in. Publishers anxious to market boys' books will often give characters manic appearances, while the covers of girls' books have a softer focus (Brennan, 1998, 50).

This pattern affects the writing of both sexes, as girls tend to choose extended reflective composition in responding to an assignment, while boys express themselves in episodic and factual detail. This is likely to result in them working with confidence on tasks that they prefer and seeing different aspects of their work as significant. Whether their preferences conform to the requirements of GCSE courses and examinations is another matter. Depending on which subject is being assessed, and the modes of expression and learning style it favours, boys' and girls' performance will be judged either 'good' or 'bad' (Gorman et al., cited in Stobart, 1992, 268).

Boys communicate less within the home, as well. They are often addicted, for instance, to computer games that communicate via symbol rather than discourse (Downes, 1994, 5). This point could have an implication favourable to boys. Being more likely than girls to own computers and use them outside school (few girls are attracted to simulated fights that involve zapping robots and monsters), they score more in surveys designed to test positive orientation to computers (Durndell et al., 1995, 219). Similarly, greater opportunities to play with mechanical toys are likely to help them do well in subjects like Physics. Science surveys conducted by the APU have shown that girls do significantly less well than boys on microscopes or stop watches. The number of instruments on which this effect may be seen increases as children go through school, so that by fifteen boys are performing at a higher level overall. Out-of-school experiences with such items contribute to boys' performance being better than girls' (Murphy, 1990, cited in Stobart et al., 1992, p 268).

Reversal of roles

This aspect takes one into deep issues regarding the effects of child rearing and socialisation. For instance, are boys under-achieving because family breakdowns are causing them to lose positive male role models? Possibly, working class boys were motivated to work hard at school in the past because they knew their futures as husbands and fathers required them to be providers. The last twenty years, however, have witnessed the demise of the traditional male breadwinner, as unemployment has worsened and the number of women petitioning their husbands for divorce has doubled.

Presumably seeing men as dispensable, women now instigate 75 per cent of all divorces in England and Wales (Cohen, 1996, 28). More children are being brought up in single-parent families. Usually, the mother is left in charge and she has to oversee the child's schooling, relegating the divorced father to the role of an occasional caller and playfellow. Survey responses in one school in Project Arianne (a Europe-wide scheme which aims to broaden adolescent male education) revealed that many boys from single-parent homes revere their mothers as role models, but not their fathers, or else they pick on footballers (Snicker, 1997, 16). Of course, there is the contrary view that the decline in fatherhood is as pernicious in its effect in two-parent families, in this case where *over*-employment is the problem. 82 per cent of British fathers with children under ten in two-parent families work an average of 47 hours a week, net of commuting time, and so probably return home exhausted and unenthusiastic about parenting, except as a weekend activity (Burgess, 1997, 3).

Linked to this situation is the fact that in infant and junior schools – and increasingly in secondary schools – teachers are usually female. Some boys are not taught by a male until the secondary phase. Indeed, by early in the next century, male teachers may have disappeared from state primary schools because of what they perceive to be poor pay and promotion prospects. The result is that boys are not so exposed to the 'masculine' dimension of some values. For instance, although males and females both compete and like to win, it is arguable that they do so in different ways: boys tend to like a more overt competitive edge to their triumphs. However able women teachers are, not all of them will find it so easy to identify from their own experience with the problems of being a boy and growing up into a young man (Meikle, 1996, 3). Also, many boys find themselves in a world of learning that is not associated with a masculine figure in their formative years: hence the activities it involves – principally reading and writing – are devalued in their eyes.

This particular concern requires sensitive treatment lest it lead to an assumption that being taught by women is somehow 'to blame' for some boys' lack of achievement (Pickering, 1997, 57-58). Nonetheless, the shortage of male role models in primary schools has been high-lighted by OFSTED and the DfEE as part of the explanation for boys having a negative attitude to schooling and it appears in international literature on this subject (see, for instance, Kimmel, 1995; Browne, 1995). Several Australian writers urge that boys' socialisation in school should be 'defeminised' so that they can form ideas of what being a man, is or should be, like. It would seek to show them how to channel their physical aggression and energy without causing harm or feeling that masculinity necessarily requires them to be tough, violent or des-tructive (Neumark, 1997, 12-13). On the other hand, not all male teachers would necessarily offer appropriate or successful role models in this respect. What is more vital, perhaps, is to have a *good* teacher, whatever that entails, of either gender to whom boys will respond positively.

Another factor that is hard to pin down is the current uncertainty and anxiety surrounding the role of the male in modern society, where employment prospects for boys are bleaker than they are for girls. Although a 'glass ceiling' is still held in place in politics and the economy by a largely male establishment, there are strong indications that the future could be a lot more female. Moves towards global free trade and innovations in technology have wiped out huge numbers of traditional male unskilled and semi-skilled jobs in labour-intensive industries like mining, engineering, building and manufacturing. The new employment markets are more akin to the dexterity, flexibility and inter-personal skills attributed to female workers, although many of these jobs are in low-paid service industries and involve much part-time work. Today, more than 20 per cent of men have female partners who are the main breadwinner (Cohen, 1996, 26). However, male employment is not diminishing because women are getting more jobs: structural employment changes are resulting in the disappearance of what have been traditionally regarded as 'real' jobs.

For those boys prepared to think about career prospects and their futures, the psychological effect is bound to be enormous. When they see what has happened to their fathers, their brothers and their extended families, it undoubtedly contributes to a reduction of motivation and self-respect in some of them. This emergence of antipathy to school and education comes at a crucial stage in their lives, especially when their female peers are no longer the victims of society's low expectations. Indeed, girls are encouraged to perform well and see careers open to them that they know were denied to previous generations. The extent to which girls from low-income households continue to suffer failure, which can represent itself in equally deleterious patterns of behaviour, has been marginalised by the present debate about boys (Plummer, 1998, 21).

So young, working-class males have to reconcile themselves to a reversal of roles. They face the loss of their traditional superiority in terms of doing the work and being the breadwinner – what they assumed was their birthright is approaching its sell-by date. And rather than embrace a 'New Man' ideal, some shattered male egos dismiss it as 'weak' and seek sanctuary in a hardened 1990s construction of masculinity that comprises 'a limited and limiting set of macho attitudes' (Grant, 1996, 6; also, see Weis, 1990; Riddell, 1992). Such 'Cave Man' role models as the tabloid media provide represent little more than loutish strength, like footballers getting drunk and smashing up anything from their wives to the interior of an aircraft. A headteacher of a school in Jarrow recently commented that 'it is better to be famous for being a clown or a toughie than working hard and being a failure... many male adults can only be important by being authoritarian' (Williams, 1996, 8). *Yobbus horribilus* rules O.K!

For many boys, then, it is not surprising that school comes to represent 'a system of hostile authority and meaningless work demands' (Warrington and Younger, 1997, 22). Researchers have noted, too, the adoption of a 'cool', anti-school pose by some African Caribbean boys as a rejection of the academic system (Mac an Ghaill, 1988). Little exists as a foil to counter their alienation and so they seek refuge in a hegemonic masculinity that threatens other boys (and girls) in school, in that those who step outside their rigidly defined gender model face ridicule. There is no formal 'men's liberation movement', no informal male equivalent of 'the sisterhood', to help them cope with their increasing loss of identity, their disaffection and their sense of hope-lessness. On the other hand, it is an optimistic sign that a recent Equal Opportunities Commission survey found pupils' perceptions of gender issues, across a range of ages and social groups and localities, are 'more open and more sensitive to changing cultural expectations and changes in the labour market than previously'. Boys also seem aware of the debate over women's working lives (Arnot *et al.*, 1996, 153).

Examinations and assessments

By the GCSE years, boys are reputed to be rather more blasé and self-assured about their prospects than girls who, on the whole, tend to be better motivated and conscientious. Boys think it is clever to boast that they have not revised and to assume everything will be 'alright on the night'. They then put their poor results down to having 'a bad day' or making mistakes (Dweck *et al.*, 1978, cited in Gipps, 1992, 283). At times, boys over-rate themselves. They think they are bright, but hide their slothfulness under a show of confidence.

Research consistently shows that self-confidence is a quality com-monly associated with boys. A survey in 1993-4 of more than 7,000 pupils, by Keele University's Centre for Successful Schools, showed that when asked to assess their own ability, more boys than girls thought they were able and fewer boys than girls thought they were below average (Barber, 1994, 8). The absence of a framework offering classroom competition and explicit rewards leads to greater difficulty for teachers in harnessing this trait. Sometimes their self-confidence expresses itself as a risk-taking or 'feet-first' attitude (Comber and Elwood, 1996, 21). Some teachers see this risk-taking form of social behaviour by boys as a rejection of their expectations (Ridley and Novak, 1983, cited in Meece and Jones, 1996, 394).

Alternatively, boys often appear more concerned with preserving an image of reluctant involvement or disengagement. For many, it is not acceptable for them to be seen to be interested in, or stimulated by, academic work. This ties in with 'goal theory' research findings that boys may use effort-minimising strategies as a way of maintaining high perceptions of ability or concealing low ability in traditionally 'masculine' subjects. It also enables them to resist the authority of their teachers in the classroom (Steinkamp, 1984, cited in Meece and Jones, 1996, 402) and has implications for the boys who still want to work, who are branded as 'swots', 'boffins' or 'keenos'.

This latter trait represents the emergence of a typology of masculinities, or even a market place in which newly adolescent boys can actually choose a style of behaviour to pursue (Connell, 1989, 295). Ethnographies of working-class schools in Britain have recorded the phenomenon's existence for some years (see, for instance, Hargreaves, 1967; Willis, 1977). The extent to which such differentiation may be the product of the hierarchical structure of a school's curriculum or its ability banding or the access given to careers and higher education – with 'laddishness' comprising the reaction of the 'failed' – has also been the subject of comment (Connell *op. cit.*).

The introduction of GCSE in 1988 brought assessment techniques – principally coursework – that have considerably improved the performance of girls and of middle-class pupils in general. Boys tended to do well in unseen, timed exams that could be passed with last-minute cramming, such as O-levels. Girls, by contrast, tend to do better with sequential assessment methods requiring high levels of sustained attention and rewarding consistent effort (Smithers, 1996, 18). Consequently, the changes brought about by GCSE have resulted in a situation in which almost all the major subjects have gender differences in outcome. They are attributable to the more diligent and plodding approach that is a characteristic of girls and the tendency of boys to produce coursework of a lower calibre because they lack the necessary application. The long haul triumphs over the last spurt (McDonagh, 1998, 16). However, coursework is not the sole agent of change, as there is evidence that girls were already improving their performance *before* GCSE was introduced (OFSTED/EOC, 1996, 7) and girls currently outperform boys in both coursework and examination components (NEAB, 1996, 7).

The question of assessment techniques goes beyond coursework, since the way in which a subject is assessed is likely to influence its organisation and teaching. There are consistent findings, for instance, that on multiple-choice exercises boys surpass girls. Boys outscored their female classmates in tests for the 1996 Third International Maths and Science Study (TIMSS), where 80 per cent of the questions were multiple-choice items (Budge, 1996, 13). Possibly it is their 'eyes down' approach that enables them to make confident selections (Harding, 1979, cited in Stobart et al., 1992, 272). Girls, by contrast, prefer more discussion and seek greater understanding before committing themselves. Not having to express themselves in written English may also enhance boys' scores. As it is, the various elements of performance assessment at GCSE, such as portfolios, project investigations, orals and coursework, do not include multiple-choice items (Sammons, 1996, 466).

There is a dilemma here. Do differences in boys' and girls' exam performance reflect real differences in attainment or bias in the types of task set? In standardised intelligence tests, it is possible to exclude items that draw on white middle-class male cultural understandings, thus ensuring that children with limited access to such influences are not disadvantaged. Similarly, examination courses scrupulously free of gender-bias in their question format, content and assessments should ensure that individuals with equal ability achieve matching results, irrespective of sex. They might also serve to encourage more balanced gender choices in certain subjects. However, if girls *strive* harder on average for high grades, and achieve them by virtue of interest and diligence, is it fair to manipulate the style of assessment to secure a balance in outcomes? Should not equality of opportunity demand 'not a substantial equality of outcome...but rather a formal equality of treatment for all relevantly like cases'? (Flew, 1986, 16)

There is the practical question, too, of how far assessment techniques that are invalid in certain contexts should be used to encourage equal outcomes. The use of multiple-choice questions in GCSE English Literature might contribute to better performance by male candidates, but would they really be a valid means of evaluating boys' perceptions of an obsessed man's sanity in *Macbeth*? The answer to this problem lies, surely, in seeking to employ a *balance* of the different types of assessment task on which boys and girls perform better respectively. Because of the different understandings, priorities and purposes boys bring to assessment tasks, they tend to interpret them differently from girls and produce different types of response. By introducing tasks so that everyone understands the desired approach and by talking to pupils about what they have produced, and why, teachers can better ensure that *all* pupils are appropriately prepared and that neither a 'male' nor 'female' version of assessment dominates (Murphy, 1989, cited in Gipps, 1992, 283).

Subject perceptions

Screening assessments for gender bias or manipulating their style addresses only part of the problem. The interaction of pupils' perceptions of a subject, the experiences they bring to a subject and the type of demands a subject makes of them exert an important influence on their choice of examination courses, as well as their performance during the courses and in final examinations. Do boys, for instance, feel awkward about pronunciation and intonation in Modern Foreign Languages, which restricts their confidence? What perceptions do their teachers have of them? Teacher stereotypes and expectations are important and may have worked to male advantage in the past, such as the effect teachers' views about boys being better at Science had on their marking of work (Goddard-Spear, 1983, cited in Gipps *ibid.*). Where teachers are aware of gender stereotypes, they find it difficult to operate entirely free of them and the likelihood is that such views are picked up by boys and girls in their classes (Comber and Elwood, 1996, 21).

The extent to which schoolchildren rate subjects as either stereo-typically masculine or feminine has been the subject of various studies, most of which reflect common findings at whatever secondary age they were undertaken. Boys' significant preferences are for Science (Physics and Chemistry), CDT, PE, ICT and, to a lesser extent, Maths. The subjects rated as 'feminine' usually include HE, English, Modern Foreign Languages, Biology, Humanities and the Creative Arts (see, for instance, Weinrich-Haste, 1981; Archer and Freedman, 1989;

Archer and MacRae, 1991; Lightbody *et al.*, 1996). Although organisational constraints that channelled boys and girls towards different examination subjects have largely disappeared from schools and although girls' achievements at GCSE are surpassing boys', there is no firm evidence of any change in these stereotypical preferences.

An important component of masculinity is avoidance of what is perceived to be the feminine, so boys in secondary school may still favour 'masculine' subjects as a way of reinforcing their identity as males, despite girls being increasingly successful in mathematical and scientific subject areas. The heart of the matter may lie in a connection between gender roles and personality traits on the one hand, and certain fields of study on the other. Parsons and Beale (1955, cited in Whitehead, 1996, 148), argued that the sexual division of labour, based on child-rearing, results in males traditionally demonstrating an 'adaptive-instrumental' role to do with manipulating the environment, while females fulfil an 'integrative-expressive' role involving the maintenance of good inter-personal relationships.

The link between these traits and some school subjects could be this: the 'masculine' ones are career-oriented and concerned with phenomena and the world of objects, while the 'feminine' ones are people-oriented, involving the expression and exploration of human emotions. Some corroboration for this lies in the research done by Rae Carlson in the 1970s into literary styles. The male style is 'distal', i.e. it represents experiences of self, others, space and time in objective and distant ways; by contrast, the female style is 'proximal', or representative of experiences in an inter-personal, subjective and immediate way (Harrison, 1996). Of course, this is all very tenuous and many would quarrel with the notion that females can cope with ideas only through the personal perspective. Evidence from cross-cultural studies suggests that differences in subject perceptions are linked to attitudes *within* particular societies, rather than innate sex differences in ability (see, for instance Klainin *et al.*, 1989; Hanna, 1989).

Perceptions may be all the boys are left with. Research based on more than 300 Australian schools, supported by comparable data from Canada and the UK, points to an 'oestrogenisation' of all subjects, including Maths and Physics. The increasing emphasis on verbal reasoning and analysing context, promoted by reforms like the GCSE and National Curriculum, puts a premium on the kind of skills in which girls have a well-established achievement and maturational advantage (Hill, 1996, 6; Pyke, 1996a, 8; Pyke, 1996b). The *application* of mathematics and the *assessment of results* in technological projects are two instances of reflective tasks that play to feminine strengths, thereby enabling them to compete with boys in subjects in which the latter had formerly held an advantage (OFSTED/EOC, 1996, 17). So changes in teaching strategy are required to help boys gain the skills necessary to develop their potential and thus offset the gender imbalance.

Unpacking the relationship between masculinities and schooling in order to determine how any of these factors affect boys' attitude and performance is a complex task, to say the least! Finding solutions for schools to apply in the form of specific and practical interventionist programmes is equally problematic. It is likely to be the subject of considerable discussion and debate for the foreseeable future. The remaining chapters in this book are intended as a contribution to that debate.

References

Archer J and Freedman S (1989): Gender stereotyping perceptions of academic disciplines. *British Journal of Educational Psychology.* 59, 306-13.

Archer J and MacRae M (1991): Gender perceptions of school subjects among 10-11 year olds. *British Journal of Educational Psychology.* 61, 99-103.

Arnot M, David M and Weiner G (1996): *Educational Reforms and Gender Equality in Schools.* Manchester, Equal Opportunities Commission.

Barber M (1994): *Young People and Their Attitudes to School.* Keele, Keele University.

Brennan G (1998): Cover-up job on the gender gap. *TES Primary.* 23/1/98, 50-51.

Browne R (1995): Schools and the Construction of Masculinity, in Browne R and Fletcher R (Eds): *Boys in Schools: Addressing the Real Issues – Behaviour, Values and Relationships.* Sydney, Finch.

Budge D (1996): Boys buck the trend and come out on top. *Times Educational Supplement.* 22/11/96, 13.

Budge D (1997): Huge gender gap in special needs revealed. *Times Educational Supplement.* 24/1/97.

Burgess A (1997): Dad's the word. *The Guardian 2.* 4/2/97, 2-4.

Cohen D (1996): It's a guy thing. *The Guardian Weekend.* 4/5/96, 26-30.

Comber C and Elwood J (1994): Gender Differences in A-Level Physics and English Literature: Is the Future Male or Female? *All-In Success.* 7 (2), 21-22.

Connell R (1989): Cool Guys, Swots and Wimps: the interplay of masculinity and education. *Oxford Review of Education.* 15 (3), 291-303.

David M and Weiner G (1997): Keeping balance on the gender agenda. *Times Educational Supplement.* 23/5/97, 23.

Downes P (1994): Bridging the gender gap. *Managing Schools Today.* 4 (4), 5-6.

Durndell A, Glissov P and Siann G (1995): Gender and computing: persisting differences. *Educational Research.* 37 (3), 219-27.

Fletcher D (1997): Why women are born to chatter. *Daily Telegraph.* 19/12/97, 9.

Flew A (1986): Clarifying the concepts, in Palmer F (Ed): *Anti-racism: an assault on education and values.* London, Sherwood Press.

Gipps C (1992): National Curriculum Assessment: a research agenda. *British Educational Research Journal.* 18 (3), 277-86.

Gipps C (1994): *Beyond Testing: Towards a Theory of Educational Assessment.* London, Falmer Press.

Grant L (1996): Under pressure. *The Guardian* 2. 11/3/96, 6-7.

Hanna G (1989): Mathematical achievement of girls and boys in grade eight: results from twenty countries. *Educational Studies in Mathematics.* 20, 225-32.

Hargreaves D (1967): *Social Relations in a Secondary School.* London, Routledge and Kegan Paul.

Harrison D (1996): Women make novel choices. *The Observer.* 12/5/96.

Hawkes N (1997): Why boys have to learn what comes naturally to girls. *The Times.* 12/6/97, 5.

Hill P (1996): *Leadership for Effective Teaching.* Paper presented at the International Principals' Institute, University of Southern California School of Education, Los Angeles, 27/7/96.

Hinds D (1995): Talking it over: how to get the boys to the top of the class. *The Independent Section Two.* 26/10/95, 12-13.

Jackson D and Salisbury J (1996): Why Should Secondary Schools Take Working With Boys Seriously? *Gender and Education.* 8 (1), 103-115.

Kimmel M (Ed) (1995): *The Politics of Manhood.* Philadelphia, Temple University Press.

Klainin S, Fensham P and West L (1989): The superior achievement of girls in chemistry and physics in upper secondary schools in Thailand. *Research and Science Technological Education.* 7, 5-14.

Klein R (1995): Tales of snips and snails. *Times Educational Supplement: Extra English.* 9/6/95, iv-v.

Kohn M (1995): In two minds. *The Guardian Weekend.* 5/8/95, 13-16.

Lightbody P, Siann G, Stocks R and Walsh D (1996): Motivation and Attribution at Secondary School: the role of gender. *Educational Studies.* 22 (1), 13-25.

Lightfoot L (1997): Attention span of boys 'only five minutes'. *Daily Telegraph.* 26/4/97.

Mac an Ghaill M (1988): *Young, Gifted and Black: Student-Teacher Relations in the Schooling of Black Youth.* Buckingham, Open University Press.

Mac an Ghaill M (1994): *The Making of Men.* Buckingham, Open University Press.

Maccoby E and Jacklin C (1974): *The Psychology of Sex Differences.* California, Stanford University Press.

MacLeod D (1997): The gender divide. *Guardian Education.* 17/6/97, 3.

Marrin M (1997): Mr Evans is right about women MPs. *Sunday Telegraph.* 9/3/97, 34.

McDonagh M (1998): Time we had jobs for the boys. *Daily Telegraph.* 5/1/98, 16.

Meece J and Jones M (1996): Gender Differences in Motivation and Strategy Use in Science: Are Girls Rote Learners? *Journal of Research in Science Teaching.* 33 (4), 393-406.

Meikle J (1996): Chips are down for Mr Chips. *The Guardian.* 31/7/96, 3.

NEAB (1996): Gender differences in the GCSE. *NEAB Standard.* Summer 1996, 6-7.

Neumark V (1997): Daddy's boys. *Times Educational Supplement* 2. 11/7/97, 12-13.

OFSTED (1993): *Boys and English.* London, OFSTED.

OFSTED/EOC (1996): *The Gender Divide.* London, HMSO.

O'Leary J and Charter D (1996): Anti-school bias blights boys for life. *The Times.* 6/3/96.

Petre J (1998): Schools plan 'action man' English for the boys left behind. *Sunday Telegraph.* 11/1/98, 4.

Pickering J (1997): *Raising Boys' Achievement.* Stafford, Network Educational Press.

Plummer G (1998): Forget gender, class is still the real divide. *Times Educational Supplement.* 23/1/98, 21.

Pyke N (1996a): Male brain rattled by curriculum oestrogen. *Times Educational Supplement.* 15/3/96, 8.

Pyke N (1996b): Is English GCSE a girls' own paper? *Times Educational Supplement.* 24/5/96.

Reynolds K (1996): He's got to be so macho. *Guardian Education.* 8/10/96, 4.

Riddell S (1992): *Politics and the Gender of the Curriculum.* London, Routledge.

Sammons P (1995): Gender, Ethnic and Socio-economic Differences in Attainment and Progress: a longitudinal analysis of student achievement over 9 years. *British Educational Research Journal.* 21, (4), 465-85.

Sewell T (1997): *Black Masculinities and Schooling.* Stoke, Trentham Books.

Smithers A (1996): New myths of the gender gap. *Times Educational Supplement.* 3/5/96, 18.

Snicker J (1997): Find a way out of the maze. *Times Educational Supplement* 2. 5/9/97, 16.

Stobart G, Elwood J and Quinlan M (1992): Gender Bias in Examinations: how equal are the opportunities? *British Educational Research Journal.* 18 (3), 261-76.

Utley T (1997): Will men ever speak the same language? *Daily Telegraph.* 13/6/97, 9.

Warrington M and Younger M (1997): Gender and achievement: the debate at GCSE. *Education Review.* 10 (1), 21-27.

Way P (1997): Real boys don't read books. *Times Educational Supplement.* 11/7/97, 12.

Weinrich-Haste H (1981): The image of science, in Kelly A (Ed): *The Missing Half: girls and science education.* Manchester, Manchester University Press.

Weiss L (1990): *Working Class Without Work.* London, Routledge.

Whitehead J (1996): Sex stereotypes, gender identity and subject choice at A-level. *Educational Research.* 38 (2), 147-60.

Williams E (1996): Despair beneath the macho surface. *Times Educational Supplement,* 15/3/96, 8.

Willis P (1977): *Learning to Labour.* Farnborough, Saxon House.

2

Helping boys do better in their primary schools

Colin Noble

Introduction

Elsewhere in this book Wendy Bradford describes the project to raise boys' achievement in Kirklees LEA. That project was, and largely still is, secondary based. It is, after all, secondary boys who have been grabbing the headlines for under-achieving academically and over-achieving anti-socially. Secondary boys are likely to be larger, noisier, more threatening, more disruptive and – worryingly – closer to adulthood. Their under-achievement is 'in your face' and the consequences can be stark and unpleasant for all concerned. However, it soon becomes apparent that if we are to tackle the causes of under-achievement, rather than the effects, we have to start much earlier than the 11-year-olds. Boys, generally, do not *begin* to under-achieve in secondary schools; they merely continue or accelerate a process that is apparent in primary schools and, often, pre-school.

Boys in primary schools display a remarkably similar academic profile to their older counterparts in secondary schools in terms of their performance *vis-à-vis* girls. In Mathematics, the girls achieve slightly better results, while in Science the boys are marginally better. It is in English that the differences appear in the Key Stage 1 SATs and continue four years later at the end of Key Stage 2. We do not know how the boys fare in the other subjects of the curriculum as, unlike Key Stage 3, there is no teacher assessment. However, anecdotal evidence suggests that, just as in Key Stage 3, girls generally do 'considerably better' than the boys.

The causes are complex and have been discussed at the beginning of this book by Kevan Bleach. In one sense it does not matter what the causes are, nor that they are often outside the influence and respon-sibility of schools. Teachers have to tackle the problems as they find them. In another sense, however, it is critical that we understand the causes as, without such an insight, we could be adopting wholly inappropriate strategies to counter them. This chapter – which focuses on boys' under-achievement in the primary school – will also occasionally link the strategies suggested to the suspected origins of under-achievement.

A three-part strategy, beginning with raising awareness

The Kirklees Project, and the resulting resources pack, suggested a three-part strategy against boys' underachievement:

- raising awareness

- whole-school, strategies

- classroom specific techniques.

Raising awareness is particularly important in the primary schools because of the staggering *lack* of insight and understanding by teachers, parents and the boys themselves. We know from teacher res-ponses to professional development opportunities, from orders for the pack from primary schools and from contact officer discussions with heads, that teachers in Kirklees and the rest of the country have not been so well-informed as their secondary colleagues about the existence of boys' underachievement. This situation is in the process of change. As LEAs and schools receive their targets for the numbers of pupils who should be achieving Level 4 in English by the year 2002 (nationally 80%), one thing will become very clear. If these demanding goals are to be achieved, then the bulk of that improvement will have to come from boys. It is simple arithmetic.

Just how to raise awareness is largely within the competence and judgement of each school. Many will find that a combination of methods will give the best results. A special newsletter home, a decision to raise the matter in *all* communications with parents, adoption of a campaign logo, parents' evenings on the issue, appointment of a governor with specific responsibilities are all tried and trusted methods. In some cases, it may be advisable not to rely too heavily on written methods but to encourage the more favoured verbal traditions of the local community: visit parents in the homes; ask community leaders to a briefing event so that they might take on the issue and its strategies through their work; ask shops, pubs and clubs to put the logo up in the window and to display the leaflets with a special helpline. Don't worry – you won't be swamped, but you are encouraging debate and understanding.

Some of the views held by parents may run counter to your aims. Some may feel that boys need, or at least deserve, a worry-free, innocent childhood where the pressures of academic achievement can be left until the 'big school'. Others may feel concerned that you are concentrating on boys at the expense of girls. It is important to persuade them that the culture of under-achievement is very hard to break once it has set in by the age of 11, and that girls stand to gain as much – both socially and academically – from your project as the boys do. Indeed, it is partially because of the under-achievement and misbehaviour of boys that girls receive less of the teachers' time and also under-achieve.

Offer strategies to parents. Encourage them to make an extra effort to get boys to share their feelings with them. Share reading time or reading activities. Make reading competitive. Ration the time spent watching television and playing computer games. Offer help in dividing homework up into small bits. Offer short-term rewards, like a kick-around or food-treat at 7 p.m. rather than a new bike at Christmas. Offer challenges such as '*Bet you can't...*' or '*Find ten uses for...*' Avoid moaning and nagging. Express admiration for other boys who try hard.

The training of school staff (not merely teachers) is also critical. Colleagues have to accept the need to change and they are not inclined to do so unless they have a clear understanding of the issues and the possibilities. If the school is to present itself as a learning organisation (see below), this should be reflected in the communications all staff have with the pupils. An interesting semantic discussion for staff is whether they see them as children or pupils? What does the answer suggest about the role of the school, or the role of their post? The remarks made to pupils by lunchtime supervisors, kitchen staff, care-takers, cleaners and all the other support staff in a school can be very powerful. Some pupils will have longer conversations with a lunchtime supervisor than they do with their teacher. They can support or under-mine the messages from the classroom and assembly. This obviously presupposes much more involvement by the support staff in whole school discussions or policies than hitherto has been the case in many schools.

Some observers have argued that raising awareness is itself all that is needed. Once the key players understand the issues, their thinking and behaviour will automatically be adjusted to encourage boys' motiva-tion and achievement. This is a sound argument, but not good enough. Raising awareness is necessary but insufficient. Evidence in Kirklees suggests that teachers and parents need two other strategies – practical support for translating their awareness into action, and an appreciation that what they are doing is the right thing for their children/pupils. It is essential that whatever you do you raise awareness first, otherwise many parents and children will not understand or sympathise with the other methods you may wish to adopt.

The three-part strategy is easy to understand – that is the beauty of only having three parts! What is very important is that whatever you decide to do about boys' underachievement is carefully planned and written down. Not only does this force the school into a serious and focused reflection, but it also serves as a well-rehearsed rationale for change and incorporates important aspects like objectives, success criteria and evaluation.

Whole School Strategies
1. English is a key issue

Not only is English the subject in which boys show most signs of under-achievement, it is the key to further learning and helps to explain why boys underachieve in other areas of the curriculum. There are a number of strategies which primary schools can adopt.

The Library: Schools should be able to consider exactly how the library could be organised to benefit boys. They often have less understanding than girls about how a library works. Giving boys responsibility within the library, explaining its functions and organisation to younger boys and showing how the library can help them in their interests are all useful ways of raising its profile and attractiveness. This can be further enhanced if the library enjoys a wider role as the resource or information centre. Boys are attracted to ICT and the library can be made synonymous with excitement and fun, which is not the image it presently enjoys in most boys' minds.

Having avoided certain stock for its focus on typically male stereotypes and interests, has the school and its library replaced such material with books which boys want to read, will ask to read, and will be excited to read? The LEA's library support service will probably have ideas about the 'right' kind of stock to attract reluctant readers, who will probably be mainly boys. Boys *do* judge a book by its cover! Choosing books with good covers, showing males as central characters is a good idea. Some schools in Kirklees have asked the boys themselves to recommend reading matter that they think might be interesting. This is sometimes non-fictional and represents boys' interests in areas like sport, computers and hobbies. Asking the boys themselves has the added bonus of securing peer group approval.

Preparation for transfer to secondary school: Secondary schools often complain that the pupils they inherit from the primary schools are not up to the standard suggested by their transfer information, particularly that they cannot read as well as had been claimed. This is often based on the introduction of a completely different menu of English by the new school which, as Graham Frater noted (1997), could almost be a different language:

...except in English, most subjects immediately make heavy demands and new demands on that [the new pupils'] literacy. They provide a diet of reading material that differs quite sharply from the staple of the primary years: it is not predominantly narrative; it is formal in style; it seldom uses dialogue; and it does not always, or even commonly, follow simple chronological order. Moreover, most subject departments require pupils to write in these unfamiliar genres with little explicit instruction. In short, stiff new challenges face the pupil whose literacy is secure.

That is to say nothing of those whose literacy is insecure! Although this observation implies that secondary schools have a lot of work to do, there is also plenty of scope here for primary schools to liaise with their local high schools and introduce and explain some of the different types of English which may be encountered within a few weeks.

Shared Reading: The idea of shared reading is not new. The value of an older pupil reading with a younger one has been well recognised for some time. In Kirklees, this has been taken further by one of our advisers. He has made a video for prospective pupil tutors which has precise instructions about how to support the younger learner. When and how to follow, lead and intervene are all very carefully explained, as is the importance of allowing the younger learner to choose the book and discuss its story and pictures. The video was not made with the under-achievement of boys particularly in mind, but some of our schools have made good use of it in this context. The pairing of Year 6 boys who are themselves low or under achievers with Year 3 boys has been very interesting. These older boys are revealed to the younger ones in roles they had not suspected. They are no longer the kickers of footballs, cock of the school and potential or real bullies, but instead are students with skills which they are willing to share and pass on to them. Some schools have claimed remarkable results, but perhaps the comments of the pupils involved are just as revealing:

I couldn't read very well but I am improving as well. I'm reading more books with George [his pupil]. I didn't like reading but now I do. (Boy, aged 11)

Sometimes when he [his pupil] has a bad day I don't enjoy it. He's made progress. When he started I thought he had to concentrate more and now he does. He reads library books without a lot of help. It helps me too. (Boy, aged 10)

My partner is learning quite quickly...now he whizzes through. I think it's interesting and I like to help him. (Boy with behavioural problems, aged 11)

When I have been teaching him, I have picked up some words, and when I used to read I was very slow, but now I can read faster. How I learned to do it, I watched a video and the video told me how to do it and be a tutor. (Boy, aged 11)

I do my tutoring with Class 5 on their mat. I ask him to read a page and if Thomas (my partner) doesn't know a word then I break up the word or ask him to look at the picture. If there is not one and he can't read the word still I tell him the word. At the end of a page I ask Thomas to read the word he got wrong to see if he could remember the word. When there's only a minute or two left I ask him to read all the words he got wrong to make perfectly sure that he remembers the words. (Boy age 11)

It is apparent that there are gains to be made through the shared reading scheme that go beyond literacy. Boys find themselves in the role of carers and teachers, and the vast majority of them say that they like it. The organisation of such a scheme is harder in a secondary school because of the disruption to a complex timetable, but some schools do manage it.

The initial training of the tutors is crucial. The potential tutors love watching the training video because it gives them a chance to be critical of 'model tutors' who show them what to do, which is the intention, and to build up their own idea of good practice and self-confidence.

2. The anti-swot culture and the school as a learning organisation

Many observers view the anti-swot culture as the pre-eminent reason for boys' under-achievement, and feel that once this question of attitude has been successfully addressed everything else will fall into place. There is a great deal of sense in this, but it is a reductionist argument. The anti-swot culture is not born of the ether. It has roots in the range of experiences boys go through which interplay with a genetic pre-disposition, the importance of which we can only guess. The overcrowded curriculum; the teaching styles in many classrooms; the systems of praise and reward; the length of tasks given to pupils; the importance given to learning and educational achievement – all inform the attitude of boys towards learning. These factors are also all within the power of the school to influence and sometimes control.

In some primary schools there is a discernible anti-work, and even anti-swot, culture by the age of seven. Whatever confusion boys may be feeling about what it is like to be a boy and what their role should be, many define themselves as being different from girls. Girls quite obviously work, *ergo* boys do not work. This poses some fundamental questions about what function boys view schools as having. It is the task of schools to ensure that they are, and are perceived to be, learning organisations. Boys should be in no doubt, as some are, that they are at school to learn. This means that the school itself has to feel that it is a learning organisation: teachers, caretakers, classroom assistants, lunchtime supervisors all have to understand their role in supporting and championing their school as a learning organisation. An anti-swot culture, more prevalent in Key Stage 2 than Key Stage 1, is a major threat to equal opportunities and should be treated in the same way as schools treat manifestations of racism, i.e. challenged at every opportunity. Schools have tended to tolerate an anti-work ethic with sighs and a corporate shrug of the shoulder. It is critical that schools challenge 'anti-swotism' both pro-actively and reactively, and at the same time reinforce the work ethic.

Primary schools are generally very good at displaying pupils' work; one only has to look around most secondary schools to realise this! Schools have the opportunity to make use of these skills directly to combat boys' underachievement and the anti-swot culture. Posters showing boys (and girls) in interesting jobs should be supported by a brief explanation of what it takes to get to that position. Last year's school leavers could either be invited back to discuss their work in the high school and how it has been helped by work in Year 5/6, and/or there could be a photographic display doing the same thing. Boys' work should be displayed even if it is not as neat or as well-presented as the girls'. The good things about the work – the ideas, the correct answers, the concepts – could be highlighted and a short commentary given about their worth.

3. The importance of role-models
Discussion about the social and educational effect upon children of one-parent families is not always welcome. Nevertheless, it would be dishonest to pretend that the million and a half families headed by a single, normally female, parent does not sometimes have a dramatic effect – both good and ill – upon the child(ren). In other contexts, I would argue strongly that it is not the structure of the family that is important but the quality of the relationships within it. However, there are a large number of boys who may not come across an authoritative adult male until they reach secondary school. Only 12 per cent of primary teachers are male, many of them heads. Eleven years is a long time to be denied a role model of what you might be when you grow up. The uncertainty expressed in some quarters about the role of the male in society is replicated, as ever, by uncertainty by school pupils. What does the eight year old think he is going to grow up to be? He knows he is not going to be his mother, and the next nearest thing which he can relate to may be a television, sport or rock music personality – a *persona* made larger than life by the popular media.

It is not just the one parent family that does not always supply the child with an adult male role model. In some parts of the country, long-term male unemployment is endemic. Again, it is sometimes difficult for the boy in the family to see a constructive role model that says something positive about the need to work and the rewards of work.

The primary school is in a position to bring male role models into the school. These could be parents of other children, older brothers or members of supporting agencies, such as police officers and fire fighters. The important thing is that they are men who show an interest in education or who can talk about education giving them a route to their success. The local football star needs to discuss the importance of education to him. If it was not, or is not, important, then do not invite him. One primary school in Kirklees organised a reading week when men were invited to read a story of their choice to Key Stage 1 and a different one to Key Stage 2. They then talked about their enjoyment of reading and what part education had played in their success.

Norfolk LEA has an advanced scheme of industrial mentoring in which local employers release their staff for about forty minutes per week or fortnight to work with, read with and talk to the students in the local schools. In Kirklees, the Council is encouraging staff to spend thirty minutes per week hearing children read, and special training has been supplied. In both cases, there are issues of child protection procedures to address, but these are not insuperable. A special effort is made to link male adults with boys.

4. Setting

In many primary schools setting will never be an issue. They are simply not big enough, even with combined classes, to contemplate it. For others, with two, three or four classes in each year, it is something they will be forced to consider.

In the 1950s students were separated by ability, or supposedly so, both within, and between, schools throughout England. The 1967 Plowden Report recommended the abolition of ability grouping in primary schools, as high-profile research showed a clear link between streaming and working class under-achievement in the secondary sector. As a result, the 1970s and 1980s saw a growth of mixed-ability grouping. The 1990s has seen a significant return to ability grouping.

Setting is becoming increasingly common in primary schools and the results sometimes suggest it has worked. The 1997 SATs, particularly at Key Stage 2, showed some significant improvements. That this often coincided with the introduction of setting is evidence enough for some schools that setting raises achievement. However, there is little doubt that other factors were at play. The realisation that they are also in the league tables strongly affected many primary heads in 1996, and they and their teachers were more thoroughly geared to preparing their children for SATs in 1997. There is no evidence that children in setted schools did any better than those that were non-setted.

For the purposes of this discussion, the equality issue relates to gender, although it obviously interacts powerfully with other aspects of stratification, such as class and ethnicity. Just as in the 1960s it was noted that, through setting, working class students sink to the bottom, so in the 1990s research shows that, through certain kinds of setting, boys sink to the bottom. They think they are probably there to stay, with their subsequent behaviour, motivation and achievement reflecting that realisation.

Suggested advantages and disadvantages of grouping pupils by ability

Advantages

- Pupils make progress that fits their abilities.

- Learning strategies can be adapted to the needs of the group.

- Interest and motivation are maintained as high ability pupils are not held back by those of lower ability.

- Slower pupils participate more when not eclipsed by those who are much brighter.

- Teaching is easier.

- Individual or small group instruction for the less able becomes possible.

Disadvantages

- Less able pupils need the presence of more advanced ones to stimulate and encourage them.

- A stigma is attached to being in a low set, which has a negative affect on motivation.

- Most teachers do not like teaching the bottom sets.

- Ability grouping discriminates against pupils from ethnic minorities and lower socio-economic groups.

- Pupils in the lower streams or sets tend to receive instruction at a slower pace and of a lesser quality than pupils in higher. They get less than their fair share of good book resources, rooms and teachers.

- The accurate and fair placement of children into ability groups is difficult. Often, a difference of one mark between two pupils will lead to a future of very different learning experiences.

- Once ability groups are established movement between groups is limited, both for practical reasons and because the self-fulfilling prophecy takes root.

The debate about setting is going to increase as more primary schools – some concerned that they may not reach their targets, others pressurised by articulate parents who like the idea – begin to adopt setting across the board or within some subjects. There is a suggestion that setting may be more appropriate in mathematics than in other subjects because it is more linear, i.e. learning depends so much more on the successful learning and internalisation of previous learning. There is no 'right' answer to the question of setting. Different schools will have different pupils, demands, traditions and teachers. Most systems work well when all involved believe in it and are prepared to work hard at its weaknesses. The question schools will need to answer when discussing their targets is this: does the system make it more or less likely that under-achieving boys will achieve better?

5. The Magic Number 8

It can surely only be coincidence, but the number eight occurs strongly in countering boys' underachievement in both secondary and primary schools. In primary schools, many teachers have noted a change of attitude of boys, particularly in Year 3 when most will be eight. The reasons are debatable, but are probably environmental rather than developmental. Evidence suggests that parents are generally pleased by their children's Key Stage 1 results, but also relieved that they are over for another four years. The same could be true of teachers, although many would dispute this.

Certainly, many parents do not read to their children as much after their eighth birthday, as they did before; even fewer continue to hear their children read. Not only are the SATs a long way off, but there is an assumption that their children can now read and further help is unnecessary. Thus, the large gains made in literacy in the infants begin to plateau for many children in Year 3. It can be likened to the novice skier who, after a few weeks of falling over and steep learning, finds that (s)he can get down most slopes in one way or another. The incentive to keep learning has been taken away. It would be interesting to know the effect of the voluntary Year 4 SATs on teacher and parental attitudes and on children's learning.

The answers to this, as in secondary schools wrestling with the torpor of Year 8 boys, are:

- to target eight-year-olds with highly public and well-supported expectations

- to explain carefully to parents the importance of their role as listeners and readers

- to set reading challenges for boys that are realistic and that stretch them

- to use phrases and techniques like 'word-attack skills' which appeal to boys' sense of competition.

Classroom strategies

1. Class Organisation

One of the most interesting pieces of work carried out in Kirklees was an experiment with seating positions in the classroom. It was felt that if a school really was a learning organisation, then that should be reflected in the classroom environment of the learner. Seating an under-achieving boy next to others of similar disposition created a comfortable under-achieving ghetto for them in which negative attitudes towards effort were constantly reinforced and valued. The task for the teacher was to think about the 'learning zone' of the pupil. This zone varied in shape and intensity, but while the pupil was at his seat it tended to be his immediate neighbours, about three others, and sometimes that corridor of communication between him and the class teacher when the teacher was addressing the whole class or talking to him individually.

Consequently, the teacher should take the initiative in deciding where individuals should sit, based not on their behaviour but on optimising their learning. This may sometimes look and feel like the same thing, but it is important that the teacher – and the class – understand that learning is the only criterion for judging seating. This policy is not without its difficulties. Some children, and some parents, may object to the lack of choice, which is why it is essential for the teacher to think it through and be able to justify the policy. It also reinforces the importance of raising awareness of the issues as the first task of any strategy adopted by schools.

Teachers have to be alert to the effects of their seating plans. Whilst it may have made sense initially to sit a under-achieving boy with two well-organised girls who are always on task and present carefully checked work, and whilst you may have explained very carefully to all three the thinking behind your decision, *is it actually working*? Is the boy beginning to learn good habits or is he disrupting them? Much will depend on the personalities of the children involved. *What must be an iron rule is that the learning of girls, or other boys, is never jeopardised by the introduction of strategies to raise the achievement of under-performing boys.*

2. Group work and short term tasks

A previous survey carried out by Kirklees LEA indicated that although many primary classrooms had pupils sitting in groups, there was very little genuine group work taking place. Most schools adopted teaching styles that veered between whole class teaching and individual learning. The question is, does this have any implications for the achievement of boys? The studies of preferred learning styles indicate that boys enjoy short-term tasks in which they are engaging with others. Obviously, there are exceptions to this generalisation, as there are with the whole issue of under-achieving boys.

The trend of the curriculum in recent years, particularly the Key Stage 2 curriculum, has been towards content-oriented work over a lengthening time scale. How else can the teacher get through the curriculum? This is a disaster for boys, as has been the narrowness of the Key Stage 4 curriculum in the high school. Boys generally respond well to short-term tasks, short term rewards and a *process*-orientated curriculum, particularly if it means working with others. Most schools will welcome the Government's announcement in January 1998 that the curriculum can be effectively slimmed down, but they may still want to cut it into bite-sized chunks whenever possible.

Boys are bored by worksheets. Schools may want to think about how to use them less, or at least more imaginatively, so that individuals within groups take on different but mutually supportive tasks, and to build in elements of challenge, not just completion. The advent of the 'literacy hour', with its very structured approach and short-term tasks, should help boys disproportionately. The plenary session at the end, with its accent on short-term learning achievements and feedback should be particularly helpful to boys if done well. Similarly, those schools which are using the First Steps scheme, which has recently arrived in this country from Australia, should find that its emphasis on a developmental continuum and teachers referring to descriptions of learning behaviours in order to assess, will also benefit boys. It is believed that both these initiatives will help reduce the differential between the genders without disadvantaging the girls which, as stated before, has to be a prime consideration of any strategy.

There are many other strategies which schools and teachers could consider. Many are discussed in the pack produced by Kirklees LEA. What is important is that any action taken is part of a well-considered plan that has the awareness and support of the school as a whole.

References

Boaler J (1996): *Setting, social class and the survival of the quickest.* London, King's College.

Bowgett D (1996): *Shared Reading Video Pack.* Huddersfield, Kirklees LEA.

Bradford W (1996): *Raising Boys' Achievement.* Huddersfield, Kirklees LEA.

Frater G (1997): *An investigation into the effective teaching of English.* London, Basic Skills Unit.

Iles M (1995): *Boys and Reading – some thoughts.* An occasional paper published by the National Literacy Trust, no.1/95.

OFSTED/EOC (1996): *The Gender Divide. Performance differences between boys and girls at school.* London, HMSO.

Piggott T, Mulvaney S and Gilleard D (1996): *Proving Improvement.* Huddersfield, Kirklees LEA.

Slavin R E (1990): Achievement effects of ability grouping in secondary schools: a best evidence synthesis. *Review of Educational Research.* 60, 471-490.

3

What difference does it make?
Factors influencing motivation and
performance of Year 8 boys in a
Walsall comprehensive school

Kevan Bleach

The situation at Sneyd Community School

For several years, test and examination results have revealed significant differences in boys' and girls' achievement. In the final year of O-level and CSE (1987), the difference between the percentages of girls over boys gaining five or more A-C grades was 1.6 per cent. By 1990 it increased to 7.6 per cent and by 1995 to 9.1 per cent (SCAA, 1996). Sneyd Community School in Walsall – an 11-18 comprehensive with 1,400 on roll – is like most English and Welsh secondaries, in that girls have usually done better at GCSE than their male classmates. In 1996, for example, 36 per cent of the girls gained five or more A*-C grades, compared with only 24 per cent of the boys. OFSTED has noted that such differences are particularly evident in urban areas where schools serve socially and economically deprived communities (Young, 1996, 4). Just under 20 per cent of our pupils are eligible for free school meals, which is close to the LEA average, but above the national figure.

In giving substance to our school aims on equal opportunities and gender, we seek to provide equal access in all learning experiences, to challenge stereotyped images and to provide for boys' and girls' particular needs. Consequently, the disparity in their academic performance is a pertinent issue. Gender is an accessible area for intervention given our ability to examine girls' and boys' results from examination board statistics. Although researchers have identified a range of explanations, the immediate concern for schools is what *practical strategies* can be set in place for improving boys' performance. The experience and expectations boys have of subjects, styles of teaching and learning, and school in general are obvious factors. Yet to delay examining their impact until the GCSE years lets negative attitudes become entrenched.

Consequently, I was pleased to lead a team of five Sneyd teachers – two English, one Maths, one Science and an LEA support teacher – in investigating these issues during the spring and summer terms of 1996. Our work was organised as a practitioner research partnership with colleagues from Wolverhampton University's School of Education and funded by Walsall LEA. We rooted our investigation where boys *begin* to show signs of under-achievement, *viz.* after the initial gust of enthusiasm in Year 7 and the early part of Year 8 begins to blow itself out. Keele University's survey of attitudes and behaviour in secondary pupils revealed that boys' motivation falls from Year 8 (Barber, 1994, 4). With the exception of recent work led by Professor Jean Rudduck, however, there is little detailed research on aspects of school life that boys of this age like or dislike, which affect their performance, and how teachers could address this problem (see Rudduck, 1995; Rudduck *et al.*, 1996). Our project was undertaken with the intention of helping colleagues improve their practice by responding more knowledgeably and skilfully to this challenge.

How we approached our research project

It was crucial to narrow the scope of our investigation to manageable proportions, given the limited amount of non-teaching time available. So we decided to gather qualitative data from semi-structured interviews, using a sample of eighteen able, but potentially under-achieving, Year 8 boys in middle-band teaching sets (there were 247 pupils in the year group). They shared class and ethnic backgrounds as our school serves a largely white and working-class area. Reports, effort grades, pastoral files, subject teachers and form tutors were consulted in order to identify our sample. After a pilot run, interviews were carried out over a two-week period with groups of two or three boys.

We thought this would provide a more balanced 'power structure' and encourage interaction between the participants.

Some of the time we used a 'critical incident' approach in our questioning to encourage the boys to offer an 'action replay' of events that reflected their attitudes to teaching, learning and school. 'Tell us about a time when...' was a common lead-in. We tried to make the sessions friendly, relaxed and comfortable in order to foster a *rapport* and avoid being perceived as distant. Confidentiality was an important ethical issue, since any concerns held by the boys formed the core of our research focus. To deepen our understanding of the underlying issues, we scoured newspapers and journals for relevant articles. Given more time and resources, we could have gone further, in terms of interviewing boys' teachers and parents, talking to *girls* of comparable age and aptitude, and engaging in pupil pursuits and classroom observations.

What our research told us
Teaching and learning activities
The first issue to emerge was that the boys did not dislike learning *per se*. What affected their enjoyment of lessons was how far they were offered opportunities for *active involvement*. It is, therefore, the *style* of teaching and learning that is crucial. The kind of activities regarded as popular included role-play, practical work and use of ICT and audio-visual aids. When these were employed, the boys were motivated to work better and, usually, felt they were more successful in their outcomes. The collaborative aspect of working together also appealed. PE was mentioned with approval, but also aspects of English and Drama:

> *I like physical things... group activities where we get up and do something.*

In the case of Drama, perhaps, it is because role-play enabled them to draw on 'real' experience, rather than have to think in a conventional cognitive sense. Practical experiments in Science also fell into this category. Indeed, one boy did not mind writing up experiments, implying that this was the reciprocal act required for the activity part of lessons.

The types of lessons disliked by the boys were passive, individual tasks that involve sitting and writing, copying from the board, reading textbooks or otherwise keeping their heads down. In this respect, Maths was generally described as 'hard' because of the large amount of writing and working out. However, where one teacher allowed games as a bonus for working studiously, this was a popular move. An active style cannot consume the whole of the Maths experience, but if more could be taught via puzzles and practical investigations, there would be a greater incentive to learn:

You'd get more involved and take part.

We know that, generally, boys grow up with an emphasis on *doing*, as well as talking. Their peer groups are competitive, with status often dependent on physical activities (Hannan, 1995). So it is understandable if they 'switch off' in the absence of sufficient stimulation. To avoid a poor rating and to hold their attention, we should consider what constitutes an effective methodology. We need only recall, for a moment, how best *we* learn on INSET courses! Traditional teaching methods cause us to use only 15 per cent of our brain when learning. How much more could be achieved by stimulating another 15 per cent through a multi-sensory approach.

A balanced and differentiated repertoire of styles, therefore, would hold greater appeal for boys' interest and imagination and serve to harness their risk-taking skills. It would also encourage them to solve problems and to work individually and as team members. This message was voiced strongly in the days of TVEI and pre-GCSE training courses: active participation and structured group work are effective instruments of teaching and learning. The strictures of the National Curriculum, however, have caused us to forget the evaluated benefits of the TVEI style: higher motivation, positive attitudes, greater maturity and better attendance (Parsons, 1993, 97-100).

Reading and writing

Despite English lessons that include weekly lessons in a well-stocked and attractive community library, half-hour reading homeworks and the provision of silent reading time in registration, the reading habits and preferences of our sample group reflected an apparent indifference to the printed word:

I don't read much... I do what I have to do and no more...It's an effort to pick up a book and read page after page... I have better things to do.

Research shows that boys in general do not read as much as girls and lack interest in the traditional types of novel. Often, the only close role models they will see reading as they are growing up are their mothers and their (largely female) primary school teachers, so reading may well be seen as a feminine pursuit. Our boys told us they disliked lengthy fiction, especially pre-1900 texts with complex narrative structures or metaphoric language. It was a 'girl thing' and left them cold. However, the actual extent of boys' reading depends on how the reading matter is defined – they are not totally indifferent to the printed word. When probed about what they *did* prefer, it was clear that our boys read magazines and information books, as well as certain types of fiction, like Christy Brown and Wilkie Collins. Favourite topics included football, computers, war, horror, action and adventure, and animals (tarantula-keeping was one cited to us), compared with the family sagas and romantic and popular fiction customarily preferred by girls. Books with pictures were also in demand:

I don't know why we can't have comic-type books in school. They do learn [sic] you something.

So one way of encouraging boys to read might be to validate a variety of reading material, even if it means investing initially in magazines, practical non-fiction, autobiographies of sports stars, television and film 'tie-ins' or science fiction. Such tastes should be encouraged within limits; for instance, certain factual material read for pleasure (on anything from computers to skateboarding) can teach familiarity with technical language. However, boys do need to be nudged into choosing reading matter of a higher order or else their tastes will languish in the purely instructional, with worrying consequences at GCSE when reflective reading is required more. Girls *already* read the reflective material that novels offer, with its emphasis on understanding character, motivation and plot.

The boys we interviewed claimed to do little reading at home, having 'better things to do' like watch television, play on their computers or go outdoors. Part of the problem, perhaps, lies in the purely physical act of lowering one's head to the page and following the lines. Many boys like social inter-action, while reading is a solitary task. The two can be reconciled in class, however, by play reading, reading aloud or peer group reading. This way, otherwise unambitious male minds could be initiated into more sophisticated tastes that will nurture their ability to be reflective. If not, they will only half-appreciate the type of reading encountered in Key Stage 4, which is a possible reason for their under-achievement at the higher GCSE grades.

Just as a gender gap appears to exist in reading habits, so there seems to be one in writing. Boys are reputed to give a lower value to the appearance of their work:

> *I start neatly, but lose control with longer pieces... Girls are neater and work harder than us... Your hand gets tired and your work gets all messy... It's an effort to do a lot of writing.*

Whether or not girls actually are neater or work harder than boys, there is a message in the above lament that longer pieces of work make it difficult to sustain a polished appearance. Boys are not necessarily deliberately careless. They tend to like quick-fire activities and step-by-step tasks, so anything involving a longer concentration span is less likely to remain neat and tidy. There is a desire to 'get it right' and move on. In our sample's eyes, there was an obvious consequence:

> *Some teachers think neat handwriting equals good work. Some of my work isn't really read and cared about... I'd like to find some other way of showing what I know.*

That other way could involve more opportunities for word processing, which would help ensure what is judged is the intrinsic quality of boys' (untidy) writing. In most state schools – unless they are City Technology Colleges – there are logistical problems caused by an insufficiency of machines. A 'lap-top' for each pupil would be ideal! When asked whether they would like to use word processors more, the boys' reactions were favourable:

> *It would make my work neater... It would be easier to please the teacher, who will think it's looking good... It helps you feel good*

about your work... It's all done for you. No Tippex – just delete the mistakes.

Another way of improving motivation would be for teachers to guard against superficial judgements of work based on its appearance. Our evidence suggests this is a single factor in stifling boys' enthusiasm and constitutes a cost factor for the learning process. If an individual's genuine effort is masked by its poor presentation, it can be destructive to fail to differentiate content from presentation when marking. More could be done, too, in heightening pupils' awareness of the types of audience for whom they are writing and the appropriate levels of neatness. English work in its draft stage, written for the purpose of discussion, obviously requires less polish than a piece of work produced for a Key Stage 3 assessment portfolio or a GCSE folder.

Homework

Little value was seen in homework or in the way it could contribute to their overall progress at their present stage of schooling:

School's the place for work. When you get home, that's your free time... Homework becomes school at home. I prefer to get my work done in the lesson... It might be useful when you're older to take work home with you.

This 'shop-floor' view that school work should be done only during the hours of nine to four is a not uncommon attitude. Most boys see homework as an invasion of their personal time, especially if they think that too much is prescribed. Setting it in a rush before the bell does not help:

Homework is handed out quickly at the end. There's not enough time to write it in our planners. I don't get it all down or I get it wrong. Why can't we be given our homework at the start of a lesson?

So they tend to do it grudgingly and as quickly as possible because, in all likelihood, they would prefer to be absorbed in their computer games or outdoors running around. A small minority operates within the defiant frame of mind that says 'we don't do homework'.

To overcome these work-frustration or work-avoidance attitudes, teachers should seek ways of modifying them in Key Stage 3. If not, they will harden and make it impossible for some pupils to complete all the ground they need for their GCSE subjects – and such a negative culture will affect boys more in terms of results. Use of a variety of homework tasks, for instance, would help counter feelings of boredom. The types that our interviewees liked included title pages for topics, research and investigations, library work, interviews, observations and any practical task, such as use of their word processors. Many homeworks are mere continuations or leftovers. The provision of extension and enrichment activity sheets or booklets for modules of work would offer a more stimulating approach and encourage an autonomous style of learning. Tasks set need not match lesson content, except in the same skill areas. At the moment, too many pupils opt out of homework. If, with parental support, an early onus is placed on them to opt *in*, their commitment to learning might be more deeply rooted by the GCSE years.

Attitudes to success and failure

Generally positive attitudes were expressed about the value of education, such as the benefits that would accrue in later life. The boys reported receiving encouragement from their parents. Certain subjects, particularly Maths, were regarded as instrumental in eventually securing employment. Others were rated as unimportant in their future value (e.g. French, Art and History), although a pragmatic justification was given for this not affecting their effort:

> We still have to follow the course, so we might as well get our heads down.

One point was clear: in addition to subjects' utilitarian value and the use of active teaching methods, their popularity derived from the extent to which boys thought they were achieving success. It is a characteristic of boys that they need to feel good and be regularly reinforced in that sense of self-esteem. They expect someone on hand to recognise their effort and offer further encouragement. Michael Barber made a point at the *Teachers Make A Difference* conferences in London and York in 1996 about praise and criticism. He said teachers should try to ensure a three-to-one ratio, with encouragement focusing on specific examples of good performance to raise expectations and develop self-esteem (OFSTED/SCAA/TTA, 1996).

Our evidence showed that where teachers recognise success and offer praise, one finds livelier participation and keener interest in lessons. When exercise books are returned, they want to see what marks have been given and particularly what comments have been written. One boy said ICT was his favourite subject because he gained most marks in it, to which his partner added that he noticed this had a snowball effect on the improvement of his friend's effort.

Conversely, they said they would be unlikely to try hard if teacher feedback was bad. This fragility of ego manifested itself in admissions of 'stupidity' and 'embarrassment', and in the desire to give up or, at least, maintain a low profile. A string of 'D' effort grades made one boy feel depressed about his prospects in Science, although he realised the only way to improve was to do better. Some teachers view a low grade as a short, sharp spur to better effort, but it is not always perceived that way by pupils whose self-confidence is more brittle than we think. To avoid resentment reinforcing poor performance, assessments should allow scope for some pupil self-evaluation and discussion with his teacher. Assessment that serves the learner is time-consuming. However, if low grades are seen simply as punishments, they are not likely to encourage the individual to do better. Higher up the school, there is the danger that some boys will regard them as a sign of 'street-cred' with their peers.

Embarrassment also arises if work is found to be too challenging:

> *All the teacher says is: 'Can't you understand it?' I feel like a thicko. I would ask a friend to explain... Sometimes you keep quiet, or wait till everyone's working and then tell the teacher if he comes over to you.*

Three boys singled out one particular 'problem' subject, especially when starting new topics. A commonly used word was 'panic'. They agreed, however, that having clearly defined steps to follow made the subject more accessible. This echoes Hannan's advocacy of 'sequencing' as a way of giving boys with lower concentration spans a structured template for any activity. It can apply to any subject, e.g. planning an English essay or writing up a Science experiment [Hinds, 1995, 12].

Public recognition of achievement did not seem to be a problem, although research shows that older boys respond better to private praise. They seemed well motivated by the school's merit system, with a couple of reservations expressed about being singled out for an award and telling their parents:

> *I've had ten merits this year – you get a certificate in assembly if you get lots. I'm not troubled about getting up to receive one if lots of kids get them... Sometimes I don't tell my mum. She just looks through my planner. But I'm pleased when she picks it up and sees what merits I've got... My mum's got to show she was interested enough to find out herself.*

Clearly, there is safety in numbers! The use of an awards assembly, when achievement in a range of areas can be acknowledged, enables a large number of recipients to be included. This is good practice, in that it encourages schools to identify and celebrate the potential for success in each individual. Also, it provides a forum in which the academically successful or hard-working boy is less afraid of being branded a 'boffin' or a 'swot' – what our pupils term a 'keeno'.

As some boys grow older, of course, it becomes less and less 'cool' to be seen to be stimulated by academic work. They tend to play down the amount of effort that they make. An image of reluctant involvement is cultivated. It also influences their attitude to other boys' endeavours. Some indication of a developing attitude in this respect was noted in our sample. Interestingly, it was made clear that one did not have to be clever to be a 'keeno' – just industrious, and obviously so:

> *They bore you. They're always talking about work or doing homework. Keenos stay in and do their work.*

When asked what is the next category down, one answer given was 'intelligent'. Bottom of the hierarchy were two other pejorative classifications: 'mongols' and 'bograts'. Presumably, most boys see themselves in-between these groups, forming a bulky 'average pupil' category. There was no evidence in the sample's responses that they associated being a 'keeno' with working like conformist girls.

While being a 'keeno' represented low credibility for some of our boys, it was by no means a strongly held feeling. A couple did not use the expression at all, despite some prompting, while several others admitted they had been on the receiving end:

> *If you want to get on with your work, they call you 'keeno'... If I do something faster, I get called a 'keeno' and asked to do the other person's work.*

The motivation of their detractors was obvious: envy and jealousy. The jibes did not bother them if they felt confident they were good at a subject or if their work mattered:

> *They don't really mean it. They're just trying to get up my nose...I call them names back... I keep going because I'm good at it and I want to show what brilliant things I can do.*

It was apparent there is not yet, at this stage in Year 8, a strong dichotomy between being socially acceptable to one's peers and being placed beyond the pale as a 'keeno'. There is schoolboy banter, but the difference is not so obtrusive as to make them recoil from such an epithet or be subject to victimisation. There was a perception that a pupil could be clever, yet *not* a 'keeno', so long as one's display of ability was not too overt. Such 'cool' cleverness is an attribute for the astute teacher to foster in boys!

For any school keen to create a more positive image about hard work and achievement, it would be worth trying to respond to one boy's comment that being in a *group* of boys who all work well offers him immunity from jibes. Again, there is protection in numbers: creating forms of classroom organisation in which pupils can share achievement with each other could develop peer group support. This would help them to be collectively proud of their efforts *and* provide a framework that enables them to maintain success and enthusiasm in the face of opposition.

Teacher-pupil relationships

The quality of teacher-pupil relationships is central to achievement by boys *and* girls. For our sample, being personable and not giving short shrift to anyone who asks for help were key traits. One teacher held in high esteem was summarised thus:

He is funny and cracks jokes. He behaves like he's our age and on our level. He entertains you, but when he says stop, we'll do our work. We're not afraid of him, but we still work for him.

The 'kind' teachers, as one boy put it, are those who allow conversation and a range of alternative tasks. They like pupils to ask questions and seek clarification. There are hints in such comments that what commands respect is a teacher regarding pupils as having individual needs and requirements. Women teachers were thought of as understanding boys more. 'Sympathetic' and 'softer' were two adjectives used. Research in Australia points to 'teacher warmth' as an important variable in influencing pupil progress through its effect on attentiveness in the classroom (Hill, 1996, 7).

By contrast, some teachers demand total class silence, explain matters just once and expect complete understanding. We got the distinct impression they sacrificed the individual to the perceived needs of the more able part of the class. One unpopular teacher was demonised as follows:

He gives out detentions. He listens to the brighter kids, which is unfair. He just moans at me for not doing as much, which is unfair. He makes us feel stupid when we can't understand work. He's sarcastic.

We were told about a French lesson, where the pupil had missed the point and the response was what seemed, to him, to be a further stream of unintelligible foreign language. The boy said he 'went all red' and felt stupid. The implication was clear: to ask questions in some contexts is to expose oneself to potential ridicule. Since this might equate with looking a 'bograt' in the eyes of their classmates, their reaction was to lie low and avoid attention. Keeping their heads down, however, is a short-sighted strategy because of its worrying implications for the progress of their learning.

Some signs were given that boys could misconstrue a flexible and 'humane' approach to classroom control as weakness:

We play up the nice teachers and give them the hardest time... We do it with a new teacher or those that won't punish you badly. It's whether you're frightened by a teacher or what he'll do to you.

When pressed on whether fear, if not pain, is a great educator, this boy said it was, although too much would make him not want to come to school. Pushed further, he confessed that 'playing up' happened when he was with a group of like-minded friends:

> *It makes you look big, look macho. I feel like a lad and make the others laugh.*

It is no surprise that boys tend to operate in a pack when they want to be disruptive. There is much more fun in playing up than being a swot, with involvement in a group serving to camouflage misbehaviour as well as keen work. Yet on their own, the bravado dissipates:

> *I play up because of my image with my friends, but then I don't want the teacher to think badly of me... I don't respect them at the time, though you do want the teacher to treat you decently.*

Teachers clearly have a subtle balancing act to make in seeking to maintain a well ordered and stimulating classroom situation. On the one hand, vigilant control is essential if they wish to avoid being perceived as weak. The personalities of some boys can be such that they need a secure framework of control, whereas girls are more sensitive to disapproval and, therefore, internalise discipline and criticism. Yet too stern and unbending an approach will alienate. Some teachers see classes as potentially hostile and lack confidence in their ability to resolve a disruptive situation. Frequent criticism and rare praise create a negative atmosphere. So do excessive use of loud reprimands, sarcasm, and aggressive reactions to minor offences. And if the male teachers are the ones who shout, it is the women, we were told, who are seen to 'nag, nag, nag'! Perhaps this is the downside of the sympathetic, 'mumsy' *persona* that some boys were quoted as liking.

Our sample particularly resented public reprimands. It was a feeling that emerged time and time again, with a strong awareness of the presence of girls on such occasions. Teetering on the brink of adolescence at this stage in Year 8, their image in front of girls is something they wish to protect strongly:

> *I hate being shouted at in front of people, especially with girls there. I'm worried what they think of me... When you have to stand*

up in front of people, they look at you and you go all red...I prefer being told off in private. You don't feel so stupid, so small.

Some boys see this last refuge of the martinet not as a sign of strength, but of weakness, and fail to be impressed by it, or they come away feeling they have been treated vindictively. We should never lose sight of the Elton Report's identification of disruptive behaviour as partly arising from some teachers' poor group management skills (DES, 1989). Yet practical in-service training in this area remains sparse, despite Elton's recommendations.

Finally, it is worth noting that some teachers were perceived as making greater demands of the boys:

Some are kinder and gentler to the girls and they talk to the girls differently... Boys get shouted at more than the girls... Teachers are harder on the boys because they find them more threatening than the girls... The boys are treated more roughly if they do something.

These responses echo research into teachers' attitudes in the 1980s when, put simply, they were reported as seeing boys as difficult and demanding, while girls were described as dutiful and teacher-pleasing (Pringle, 1996, 16). If teachers do tend to behave in this way, possibly reflecting their schools' generalised expectations, it reinforces rather than breaks the stereotypical mould of the 'naughty boy' and the 'virtuous girl' (Graham, 1994, 16). In the eyes of our boys, such indulgence is mis-placed. The girls do their work and listen and pay attention and understand better, which the boys do not always manage, but they actually 'talk more than the boys'.

Would boys-only sets be an answer? Several media features have made this the focus of their investigations into boys' under-performance and claimed that single-sex arrangements are better for girls and boys. Different strategies could then be employed to enable boys to respond to 'short term goals, visual stimuli and quick fire activities', while 'more reflective' work can be done with the girls (Slater, 1996, 26). Our sample of boys saw no particular virtue in segregation. Their opinions ranged from being 'not really bothered' to a firm rejection of the idea as it 'wouldn't seem right'. One volunteered the view that he was pleased to be with girls in Drama because he worked 'harder and better'!

What has our research project taught us?

Our research was carried out in a school with a well-established pastoral system and a 'culture of success' which encourages all pupils to have high expectations. It did not surprise us to find that our potentially under-achieving boys actually see the totality of their educational experience as reasonably pleasant. School was not alien to them, they did not wish to fail with their work and they did not want most of their teachers to think badly of them.

Year 8, however, is a turning point when, for some boys, a downward slope becomes the easy option. It is not, as Michael Barber rightly observes, 'the inevitable consequence of adolescence' (1994, 5). There are the extrinsic factors, which arise from nature and nurture and the type of society we live in. However, many of the changes in attitude which lead boys to start mucking about at the back of the classroom are substantially rooted in the educational challenges, the quality of teaching and learning, and the nature of pupil-teacher relationships in any institution.

The latter part of Year 8 is the point when a number of potentially pernicious influences intrude. The novelties of being members of a new school have gone and engagement can flag; new social groupings have been formed, sometimes to the detriment of work; and their emerging adolescence makes them question patterns of conformity their schools expect. Failure to address such issues can cause boys to 'turn away from learning' (Rudduck, 1995, 5), with the corollary of poor effort and behaviour, GCSE results that trail behind girls, and a failure to secure employment or post-16 training opportunities. The last thing schools need is an educational under-class of disfunctioning, disaffected boys.

So strong, now, is the awareness of this problem that various schools and LEAs are trying different approaches to counter under-achievement in boys. It is a welcome move, considering how little attention has been given in recent educational reforms to what should lie at the heart of education – pupils and their learning. Partly this may be because it is difficult to change teaching practices influenced by the pressures of the National Curriculum, partly because such changes are less tangible than, say, testing and so lack immediate political appeal (Levin, 1996,

8). From our research findings, we identified five broad areas for working to maintain an interest in learning and achievement in our school's adolescent male population. Some involve practical steps, while others imply a more fundamental shift in thinking. None offer simple solutions, given the wider contextual social circumstances affecting some boys' performance.

■ **Develop more activity-based or experiential approaches to learning**. Substantial progress is likely to be made only if styles of teaching and learning are a top priority in school development plans and INSET programmes. The works of Piaget, Vygotsky, Bruner and Gardner regarding how children learn should be consulted as possible frameworks for developing different learning opportunities. The use of lead lessons, team teaching and lesson observations are invaluable in sharing good practice. Of course, the formal constraints of GCSE courses must be recognised as essential complements to any enhancement of the active and experiential side of learning, but teachers must be encouraged to explore methods that extend beyond those they find most comfortable or quick to prepare.

■ **Target reading and literacy skills.** Reading has a great value for all kinds of learning, so a positive and invigorating environment should be encouraged to counter boys' tendency to read less than girls. Private and public reading opportunities, collaborative book reviews, use of CD-ROMs, book weeks, visiting authors – these are the kind of activities that raise the profile of reading with boys. Investment in information technology will provide boys with greater opportunities for word processing, thereby helping them give their work a more professional appearance and realise that good presentation is an integral part of the learning task.

■ **Review the nature and purpose of homework**. Homework clearly benefits pupils' education and it is one of the main concerns of parents when selecting a secondary school. Its nature and structure should be reviewed, therefore, in order to make it seem more worthwhile to those who are the direct consumers – the pupils. Rather than maintaining a vestigial existence as an old, established school procedure in which boys are expected to comply merely as obedient servants, homework should be used to develop autonomous learning and the further practice of *skills* learnt in the classroom. It should involve a variety of tasks, including investigations, observations, reading, drawing, problem-solving, use of local community facilities, etc.

■ **Celebrating success and creating a climate for achievement.** We must search constantly for ways of celebrating boys' successes, with the aim of showing them that we recognise in each individual the potential for some kind of success – whatever their own wish to play down the effort they make. We would then witness a shift in attitudes away from 'you must not be seen to be trying' towards 'I know what I'm actually worth' (Robbins, 1994, 1). It goes without saying that rewards and recognition should be of a type held in esteem by boys of particular ages, so some market research on this point would be appropriate for schools.

■ **Positive classroom and behaviour management.** Teachers' behaviour management skills are probably the single most important factor in achieving quality standards in the classroom. It is crucial, therefore, to help staff create a positive and structured teaching and learning environment by implementing methods of behaviour management that put a strong emphasis on praise, motivational challenge, effective communication, and rewards for good behaviour as well as good work.

Various other approaches are being explored by schools for encouraging boys to maintain a positive attitude. These include:

• using sixth-formers for paired reading with younger boys

• personal teacher-pupil reading interviews so that praise can be personal and not embarrassingly overt

• monitoring gender balance in teaching sets

• giving boys a high profile in showing visitors around

• celebrating boys' achievement in displays

• including their work in exemplar portfolios of attainment target levels

• pairing boys with girls in group work to expose them to 'feminine' skills of language and reflection

- involving them in marketing subjects at GCSE and post-16 recruitment evenings

- ensuring equal boys' representation on year or school councils

- exploring gender stereotypes via the curriculum

- securing parental support (Bleach, 1996, 17-19).

Implementing only a proportion of these suggestions requires considerable vision, leadership, staff commitment, in-service training and resources. Vision and direction are necessary to establish and pursue goals and priorities. Commitment is essential to engage the great majority of staff, rather than a dedicated few. Their capacity to respond effectively will be strengthened by investing in professional development opportunities and appropriate resources.

One cannot predict with certainty that any measures will *guarantee* the improvements in boys' opportunities and performance. An important *caveat* is that nothing must be done which would have the effect of restraining girls' opportunities. Nevertheless, having pinpointed at the start of our research a state of affairs that we wished to improve on, our subsequent work revealed to us certain amenable fields for action in terms of preventing our boys becoming the 'lost boys' of newspaper headlines. We problematised where it was feasible, taking as the starting point the boys' own accounts of their experiences. That is why we identified no more than five key areas for negotiated improvement within our institution.

If this modest initiative in school improvement helps our younger boys develop and sustain 'a sense of the importance of learning' (Rudduck, 1995, 3), which will carry forward into their option choices and GCSE courses, then we shall be very satisfied. Initial signs are encouraging: in our GCSE results last summer (1997), 29.6 per cent of girls gained five-plus A*-C grades, while 30.2 per cent of the boys were successful in this respect. Only time will tell if we are genuinely making progress in improving boys' attitudes and performance.

Acknowledgements

I wish to thank Ann Green, Jill Smith, Tom Blagden, Mark Gutteridge and Brian Hepburn of Sneyd School for assisting me in this investigation, and Dave Ebbutt, Colin Fletcher and George Bramley, all formerly of the University of Wolverhampton Educational Research Unit, for their practical assistance with research techniques.

References

Barber M (1994): *Young People and Their Attitudes to School*. Keele, Keele University.

Bleach K (1996): Boys Will Be Boys – But Will They Be Successful? *All-In Success,* 7 (2), 17-19.

DES (1989): *Discipline in Schools* [The Elton Report]. London, HMSO.

Graham J (1994): *Gender Differences and GCSE Results*. Keele, Keele University.

Hannan G (1995): Improving Boys' Performance Theory. *Improving Performance* computer disk. Much Wenlock, Geoff Hannan Training International.

Hill P (1996): *Leadership for Effective Teaching*. Paper presented at the International Principals' Institute, University of Southern California School of Education, Los Angeles, 27 July 1996.

Hinds D (1995): Talking it over: how to get the boys to the top of the class. *The Independent Section Two*, 26/10/95, 12-13.

Levin B (1996): *An Epidemic of Education Policy: What Can We Learn From Each Other?* Paper presented to the Canadian Association for the Study of Educational Administration, St Catherine's, Ontario, 5 June 1996.

OFSTED/SCAA/TTA (1996): *Teachers Make A Difference Post-Conference Report*.

Parsons C (1993): TVEI and the Appeal of the Really Useful Curriculum, *Evaluation and Research in Education*, 7 (2), 93-105.

Pringle M (1994): Single Sex v Co-Ed – Revisiting the Debate. *All-In Success*, 7 (2), 16.

Robbins J (1994): *Celebrating Success!* Weymouth, The Talent Centre Ltd.

Rudduck J (1995): *What can pupils tell us about school improvement?* Keynote address to the ISEIC Conference, London Institute of Education, 6 October 1995.

Rudduck J, Chaplain R and Wallace G (Eds) (1996): *School Improvement: What Can Pupils Tell Us?* London, David Fulton.

SCAA (1996): *GCSE Results Analysis*. London, SCAA.

Slater A (1996): The lost boys. *Managing Schools Today*. 5 (9), 24-26.

Young S (1996): Girls on top after three decade climb. *Times Educational Supplement*, 10/5/96, 4.

4

Boys and literacy
Effective practice in fourteen secondary schools

Graham Frater

Introduction

This paper is concerned with boys' literacy, but carries clear implications for the teaching of boys and girls alike. It is a report of effective practice in 14 mixed secondary schools in a survey commissioned by The Basic Skills Agency. The paper falls into three main sections: it shows how the needs of three target groups were addressed by means of whole school initiatives and through the policies and practices of special needs and English departments. The schools, in urban, suburban and rural areas, were visited during the summer term in 1997. They served pupils aged 11-16, 11-18 or 13-18. Most were comprehensive; no single sex schools were included, nor any selective schools serving able pupils alone. The target groups, covering the whole ability range, were: pupils with special needs; pupils whose literacy is below average, but who are not served by the special needs department; those of average achievement and above.

The survey took place against a background of public anxiety about standards of literacy. And most of the head teachers and special educational needs co-ordinators (SENCOs) in the survey schools noted that the average reading scores of their new entries of pupils had declined over a four or five year period – sometimes dramatically. They were clear that the cause lay less in methods for the initial teaching of reading than in the reduced time available for reading in an overcrowded primary school curriculum. In a recent report on 37-year-olds, The Basic Skills Agency has shown that the negative effects of failing to become securely literate at school can be both profound and enduring – and that they are increasing:

> *Whatever has gone wrong in education that led to these difficulties in the first place, **maintains its impact throughout adult life – We have to conclude that the difficulties associated with these problems have intensified over the years*** (Bynner and Parsons 1997, 79, 83, my emphasis).

These associated difficulties include unskilled occupations, low pay, a lack of advancement and training at work, bouts of unemployment, poor health, depression, rented housing (as distinct from home ownership) and, for men, a divorce rate that is markedly higher than for those whose basic skills are secure: 40 per cent *cf* 16 per cent (Bynner and Parsons 1997, 61). In addition, poor literacy is found in more than one in two prison inmates, compared with one in six in the general population (The Basic Skills Agency 1994, 16), and most convicted prisoners are male.

The factors underlying the perceptible differences between boys' and girls' achievements in literacy are complex and varied. They probably include a biological dimension; they certainly include a wide variety of interlocking social elements. However, it is equally plain that schools can and do make a difference. That they do so is shown by the cyclical inspection system and in the literature of school improvement: both show that schools serving closely similar intakes of pupils can produce contrasting results. Though all were at an early stage in their programmes, the schools in this survey also showed that, without hindering the achievements of girls, boys' achievements in literacy could be improved and that the gap between boys and girls might also be reduced.

Whole school approaches

1. Baseline testing

The survey schools demonstrated the value of baseline testing for each year's entry of new pupils. All the survey schools used some standardised tests, usually as a means of identifying pupils with special needs. The most common were standardised reading tests, often in conjunction with similar tests of spelling. Several schools used more elaborate forms of initial assessment, frequently as a means of measuring later progress and the value added by the education they were providing. No schools made significant use of national assessment data from the end of Key Stage 2: staff felt that the information could not be relied upon and that it lacked useful diagnostic evidence.

Where policy and practice were most developed, the evidence from baseline testing was used not only to identify pupils with special needs, but to pin-point underachievement. Commonly, the results of a standardised test of cognitive ability (usually non-verbal and/or verbal reasoning) were compared with information from standardised reading and spelling tests. The sharpest discrepancies were usually among boys. Targeted help was offered to pupils whose literacy scores were significantly below their more general test results. Whether having special needs or not, they could be offered systematic support and encouragement, often on an individual basis.

2. Targeting, monitoring and mentoring

With the evidence of baseline testing to hand, several schools had developed lively initiatives for tackling underachievement for groups and individuals alike. These included:

- sharing assessment data, including predicted examination grades, with pupils and parents

- assemblies where school and national examination results are discussed, including the trends of boys' achievements

- occasional single sex assemblies, as above

- regular staff meetings where the achievements of individual pupils are discussed in detail (with data sheets to hand that record potential, norms and progress)

- the use of mentors for targeted pupils (e.g. selected staff members, sixth formers and, where a business partnership scheme is in place, members of local companies)

- individual meetings between pupils and tutors, (or with appointed mentors), reviewing progress in the light of explicit data

- the award of merit certificates

- the establishment of homework and revision clubs

- the involvement of the local TEC, including as a provider of speakers, funds and mentors.

CASE STUDY: 11-16 comprehensive school
Resources for Y11 tutors for 1:1 interviews with pupils, following their mock GCSE examinations.

You will have:

1. A full copy of the post-mock examination report grades for each member of your tutor group.

2. A set of red bar charts showing predicted grades which will be issued to members of your tutor group (predicted grade: the grade a student is likely to achieve if s/he continues to work as at present).

3. A duplicated copy of grey bar charts for all members of your form which includes the following information *not shown on the student's chart*:

   - NFER score – shown on the bottom left corner of each graph. This is the total SAS (Standardised Age Score) from the three tests taken by students when they were in Years 7 and 9. In general, the lowest score possible is 210 and the highest score is 390.

   - A target points score that is mainly derived from a consideration of NFER score, but which also pays attention to the student's current level of performance.

   - A target points distribution, such as 'All subjects at six points or above', or, 'Five subjects at 5 points, 5 subjects at 4 points'. (A* =8, A=7, B=6, 0-5, D=4, E=3, F=2, G=1). If a student is predicted to get an unclassified grade this will not show on the graph.

   - Some students' graphs also have a pencil asterisk that indicates underachievement when current performance is compared to potential. In these cases the target points total may look much higher than the current points total. These students have a lot of work to do!

4. A set of duplicated sheets entitled 'Where can I improve?'

3. Teaching quality

Where schools had been most effective with boys' literacy, explicit attention had been paid, as a matter of overall policy, to teaching methods and techniques. Unsurprisingly, these were often schools that had been commended for effective teaching in a recent OFSTED inspection. There were two clear strands to these developments:

- all departments were encouraged to consider and develop their teaching approaches

- the trend of the subsequently developed methods and techniques was both to increase the specificity and coherence of lesson delivery and to place greater responsibility on students for their own learning.

Among the ways in which heads and senior management teams encouraged the development of teaching methods were:

- the provision of a series of school-based in-service training sessions (where teaching method was the centre of attention and where departments, in rotation, shared their approaches)

- the development of a tradition of classroom observation – quite distinct from the teacher appraisal scheme – both within and between departments and by members of the senior management team attached to particular departments or faculties

- at regular intervals, the posing of questions about teaching issues *for written answer and a given deadline* to all subject departments; such questions included:

  - how does your department seek to motivate pupils?

  - how does your department help pupils with note making?

  - how does your department make practical use of the assessments it records?

  - how does a typical lesson in your department begin?

Among the teaching approaches that developed as a consequence of such encouragement were:

- brisk starts to lessons, with objectives clearly shared and stated

- a well maintained and appropriate pace

- lesson endings that review what has been accomplished

- varied activities in lessons in clearly phased stages

- varying the seating arrangements and groupings during a lesson

- high expectations related to specific tasks, combined with a non-confrontational approach to discipline

- jig-sawing (dividing responsibility for parts of an overall task among groups of pupils, and making each group responsible for an outcome to the class as a whole)

- regularly using grids, columns, spider diagrams, flow charts and other graphic aids to thinking and to the structuring of ideas

- being explicit in setting and modelling written assignments, and pre-viewing effective examples of the task, style or genre required

- using systematic approaches to handling and interrogating texts and to guiding written work (see more fully under English below)

- sharing headings, structures and sentence stems for note-taking, but avoiding dictation or copying.

It is a list that could be extended beyond endurance; however, a helpful set of criteria, and hence of further ideas, may be found in OFSTED's handbook for secondary school inspections (HMSO, 1995).

4. An awareness of boys' needs

The most effective schools had set out less to boost the achievements of boys alone than to address underachievement in general; under-achieving girls were offered the same kinds and amounts of support. However, boys were by far the predominant underachievers and in-service training on the theme of the underachieving young male had often been provided. Rather than leading to narrowly focused approaches, this training had had the general, and probably more useful effect of raising teachers' overall awareness. In some schools, small working parties of staff had gathered and presented research materials and press cuttings to their colleagues. LEAs can be especially helpful by providing training, promoting awareness and with the dissemination of well-founded evidence. There was clear evidence of such effective support from West Sussex, Warwickshire, Kirklees and from both the Birmingham LEA and Birmingham's Roman Catholic Diocese. There was also some indirect evidence of the good influence of materials developed in Shropshire and of those disseminated by the School Curriculum and Assessment Authority (SCAA).

5. *Groupings*

Whilst a culture of awareness and well-judged concern is essential for addressing boys' achievements, the best form of organisation is much less clear. Among the survey schools, setting, mixed ability teaching, single sex teaching and structured mixed sex groupings were used; each school found success in its own approach. Most of this experimentation occurred in English classes and will be discussed more fully below.

Nonetheless, setting was the most common form of organisation and a clear general warning was sounded by a number of heads and teachers. Their message was that with the strictest forms of setting – on the basis of previous achievement alone – the top sets would be nearly all female, the lower sets all male *and demotivated*:

> *Boys must be able to feel in touch with the game.*

> *All our classes up to Year 10 are mixed ability and **they stay quite broad in Years 10 and 11**. Therefore, there are good role models for boys in the way girls work. **They are not dumped in bottom sets**.*

> *Broader band setting gives boys access to higher grades without attracting stigma.*

> *Boys are regarded as higher achievers [i.e. when placed in higher sets], so they achieve!*

Most of the schools that used setting held similar views and took a broad-brush approach to their arrangements. There was no evidence that such arrangements hindered the achievements of girls. There was some evidence that when the setting arrangements that suit one subject are permitted to determine those for another, inequities and inconsistencies can easily arise and may affect standards of achievement.

Special needs departments

1. The challenge of poor literacy in the secondary school

It is common to find a twofold disjunction between the literacy acquired in the primary school and that required by the secondary. First, despite clear evidence to the contrary, the secondary curriculum requires schools to assume that the literacy of *all* their new pupils is secure. Secondly, except in English, most subjects immediately make heavy new demands upon that literacy. They provide a diet of reading material that differs sharply from the staple of the primary years: it is not predominantly narrative; it is formal in style; it seldom uses dialogue; and it does not always, or even commonly, follow simple chronological order. Moreover, most subject departments require pupils to write in these unfamiliar genres with little explicit instruction. In short, stiff new challenges face the pupil whose literacy is secure.

When a pupil with insecure literacy starts at secondary school, both he (commonly) and his school face a peculiarly severe set of challenges. The pupil has often reached a point where he is aware of his problems; he may also stand in danger of becoming anxious or disillusioned. At the same time, he must improve his basic skills and keep up with the growing demands that new lessons make on his old weaknesses. In turn, against the thrust of its timetable structures, against the clock, and still teaching all the new content of the National Curriculum, his school must help him to progress. If he does not catch up fast, he will become increasingly disadvantaged. As he grows older, there is every danger that, if his problems persist, he will become demotivated, develop behaviour or attendance problems and fall further behind – or even drop out all together.

The reading difficulties of the SENCO's clients commonly began in their early years. They are often pupils who did not catch on to initial reading effectively and did not, therefore, read as much as their peers. As a consequence, they did not reinforce their insecure skills. Marie Clay has shown that, by the end of the first year of primary education, the number of words read in school by a proficient new reader can be four times greater than by a child who is making a poor start (Clay 1991, 209.). It is a gap that widens rapidly throughout the primary years (Sylva and Hurry 1995, 2). And the good reader, by reading at home, will widen it still further. Moreover, the secondary school curriculum is probably more steeply incremental than the primary. These are the challenging contexts in which the gap must be closed in Key Stage 3. In addition, no matter how explicitly the basic skills are taught again by the secondary school, pupils who have fallen badly behind in reading are not likely to consolidate their skills unless the school also provides for the reading practice they have missed.

To varying degrees, the special needs teams in the survey schools addressed these challenges explicitly.

2. Parents

All the survey schools kept parents informed about their children's progress and about the help they were receiving. Several went further and sought to involve parents directly. One SENCO regards parental support as a condition of successful progress. He calls a meeting for the parents of the failing readers in Year 7 as soon as he has completed his screening tests. He shares the problem with them. In particular, he seeks their co-operation in listening to their children's reading for not less than ten minutes every day. He also seeks their agreement to maintain frequent contact with him by means of a reading notebook that passes back and forth between home and school. He finds that the parents are usually grateful to be informed and that their support is crucial. Sometimes they are surprised and wonder why they had not been asked to help before. Though rare, he notes that when a parent refuses to co-operate little progress occurs and that his other strategies for supporting the child seldom thrive.

The daily involvement of parents is one means of addressing the backlog of reading experience noted above. It is perhaps equally important as a signal of parental support and concern. With or without holding an initial meeting, other survey schools followed similar strategies for seeking parental engagement; these included:

• an advisory leaflet on hearing pupils read at home

• communication about merit points awarded for effort and progress in reading

• 'graduation days' when pupils leave the reading support programme.

3. Multi-layered support

Independence in reading is not achieved by learning letter-sound relationships. It is a much larger cognitive enterprise relating to thinking and understanding and governed by feedback and self-correction processes (Clay 1991, 254).

A single strategy is unlikely to succeed with the interlocking difficulties that poor readers experience in the secondary school. The survey schools had all recognised the need to tackle literacy in a variety of co-ordinated ways. Some schools used many of the approaches listed below; others used a smaller selection. The strategies shown in italics were common to nearly all the survey schools. The approaches included:

- *withdrawal teaching for small groups*
- *in-class support by qualified teachers and/or special needs assistants*
- *paired reading schemes – using volunteer help from teachers, parents, school librarians, dinner time assistants, older pupils, adults from local partnership companies, and others*
- *parental reading partnerships* (as in **Parents** above)
- one-to-one revision and review sessions, once a week (or once per timetable cycle), with a special needs assistant
- using special needs staff to teach the bottom English sets
- literacy software programmes for older students, used outside normal school hours
- a 'buddy' system (in which an abler pupil regularly assists a peer)
- a lunch hour spelling club
- a homework clinic that offers help with organisation and with interpreting set tasks
- a lunch time scrabble club (mostly attended by boys)
- a revision club.

4. Intensive literacy teaching

As the child fell behind his or her peers, the prospect of catching up became increasingly remote (Bynner and Parsons 1997, 35).

The survey schools had clearly recognised the need to accomplish rapid progress for their new entries of weak readers. Most had made withdrawal teaching in Key Stage 3 – especially in Year 7 – central to their strategies. While withdrawal is not itself uncommon, several of the survey schools were relatively unusual in giving it such emphasis. In these schools in-class support was usually a supplement to withdrawal teaching for the weakest pupils; elsewhere, it is common to give in-class help the greater emphasis.

In-class help is undoubtedly the appropriate course for pupils with physical or sensory handicap and often for behavioural problems too. Where literacy is the chief difficulty, in-class help frequently has the drawback of being diffuse, contingent and inefficient; for example, whenever plenary teaching occurs, the classroom helper is necessarily inactive. With priority given to the subject teaching that is going on in the lesson, the pupil's specific difficulties with literacy can seldom be given either close or consistent attention. Instead of promoting independence, it is help that can readily create dependence.

There are many practical difficulties to withdrawal work, the greatest perhaps is the disruption of the subject timetable. In effect, the most vulnerable pupils face the added difficulty of catching up with the subject teaching that they lose when they are withdrawn. Withdrawal work must, therefore, be as efficient and short-term as possible. The survey schools did not have the resources to provide the most tightly differentiated help, namely one-to-one literacy teaching. They worked with small groups, usually of about eight to twelve pupils, in brisk and tightly structured lessons on common tasks. Their chief emphasis was on reading aloud: they used carefully graded texts. Some schools used a commercially published kit in which meaning receives little attention. They wisely made up for this deficiency by emphasising discussion, by pre-viewing the vocabulary and its meanings, by using phonic, contextual and other cues when a pupil became stuck and by warmly praising pupils' self-corrections. Several schools set clear targets for these groups: they aimed for two years' gain in reading age before the end of Year 7. They were usually successful and sometimes made the gain much more rapidly.

CASE STUDY: 11-18 comprehensive school
Special needs policy and practice

A recent OFSTED report described this as a 'good school'. It noted that: (i) 'Those with statements of special educational needs make good progress throughout Key Stage 3' and that (ii) 'The progress of lower attaining pupils is appropriately maintained in Key Stage 4 in the core subjects of English, mathematics and science'.

The overwhelming aim of the team is that pupils should make a rapid progress and be able to proceed independently with the National Curriculum.

Some key features:

* *A core programme of withdrawal for group teaching for 10% of the timetable for the weakest readers.*

* For one lesson per 10-day timetable cycle, each pupil is given a one-to-one lesson with a member of the SNA team. This is a structured session of revision and review on the work he has covered during the cycle. Targets for the next cycle are also set. As reported, all pupils enjoy this lesson, not least for the individual attention it affords, for the reinforcement it offers and for the opportunity to acknowledge clear progress together.

* In-class support is also part of the scheme. Each SNA works with the same pupil(s) in each support lesson; the SNA and the host teacher are each provided with a simple diagnostic account of the problems experienced by each pupil on the register.

* A paired reading scheme, using older students (they have been offered an element of training by one of the SEN teaching staff) is also part of the provision.

* The progress of all pupils is closely monitored. *Pupils are discontinued from the withdrawal element on a termly basis, as they meet targets.*

* Good record keeping is essential to the scheme. Regular testing is used and simple record sheets maintained.

English Departments

1. A note on context

English departments are concerned both with the basic and the advanced skills of literacy. Pupils of average ability and above need to continue to develop their skills. Pupils with special needs generally attend English classes at least as often as they receive special help. And the English team is, in addition, chiefly responsible for tackling the poor literacy of a large penumbra of underachieving students who are not assisted by the SEN team. Just how severe these latter problems can be was illustrated by one 11-16 school where limited resources dictated that the cut-off point for SEN help was placed at a maximum reading age of 8.5.

The English departments in the survey schools were acutely aware of the problems of low achievement and of the negative attitudes to reading and writing of many boys. Most English teams were wholly or predominantly female. Since this was a survey of good practice, most were also unusually effective with boys, some outstandingly so.

2. Paired, silent and voluntary reading

I quickly learned that reading is cumulative and proceeds by geometrical progression: each new reading builds upon whatever the reader has read before (Manguel 1996, 19).

All the English teams recognised the need to consolidate basic skills by boosting the reading experience of their underachieving new pupils. Often in partnership with their special needs colleagues, they too organised paired reading schemes to match experienced and adept readers with underachievers in Key Stage 3. This provision could seldom be timetabled; it was an extra and voluntary activity and consequently varied in its frequency. There was no evidence of unnecessary duplication between SEN and English colleagues. Several departments made a special point of recruiting capable older boys to pair with younger and weaker ones, sometimes with dramatically positive effects.

To support pupils of all abilities to the end of Key Stage 4, many English departments also built a regular period of silent reading into their timetables. The time that was reserved varied between schools; some began each lesson with ten minutes of silent reading, some gave it one lesson a week. Most had also established a simple form of reading record for pupils to maintain; it allowed teachers to monitor choices and make new suggestions. On an occasional basis, some schools encouraged pupils to share this reading in whole class lessons with snappily written book reviews for a teenage readership, with oral reviews and with video presentations. The organisation of book clubs and book purchasing schemes helped to reinforce this emphasis and to give pupils pleasure in the possession of books.

Inevitably, there was an overlap between structured occasions for silent reading and reading as a leisure activity. In general, the effect was to boost voluntary reading. Some schools, through the school library's computer software, were able to monitor the effects of their encouragement. A clear measure of effectiveness was found if the borrowing patterns – which are often lively in Years 7 and 8 – were actively maintained in Year 9, and especially into Years 10 and 11. With some library software it is also possible to monitor borrowing both by gender and individually.

CASE STUDY: 11-16 comprehensive school
A paired reading scheme

- *Offered to a wide group of underachieving readers who do not receive withdrawal teaching.*

- Sessions occur twice weekly, usually during registration or assembly.

- The supporting listeners include volunteer parents, dinner ladies and a selection of Y10 pupils, including some boys. An element of training has been provided by the SENCO.

- *Texts are carefully chosen for the scheme and held in trays – all have been colour-coded by levels to support progression.* Each pupil has been assigned a book or level and his own copy awaits him in his tray.

- Some grant money was obtained to buy the texts for this project.

This Case Study was included to emphasise the importance of selecting texts effectively. Observation during inspection suggests that a common weakness lies in the selection of inappropriate texts, often over-ambitiously, by pupils themselves. Well-judged guidance is essential; this applies equally to home reading programmes with the parents of pupils with SEN.

3. Teaching advanced reading skills

The illusion that the teaching of reading is the concern solely of the infant school should be dispelled, and in a most positive way (Walker 1974, 12.)

In most survey schools English teachers paid closely planned attention to the advanced reading skills specified in the National Curriculum. Inspection experience suggests that this degree of systematic attention, combined with the clarity and ingenuity of the approaches used, is still relatively unusual. A thread of common practice lay in their deployment of a number of techniques that may be used with pupils of widely varying abilities. These were the Directed Activities Related to Texts (DARTS) whose effectiveness was evaluated and promoted by Nottingham University nearly two decades ago (Lunzer and Gardner 1979; 1984). Their worth is gaining recognition once again. The techniques include group prediction and deletion activities and cannot be described in detail here (but see the list of references). Walker contrasted these approaches with the traditional test of comprehension. He noted that the reading practices underpinning advanced skills are:

Forward-looking, anticipatory and predictive, active and questioning, and the attitudes essential to reading of this order are unlikely to be developed by backward-looking procedures where reading is reduced to passivity and mere recall by questions which are asked when all has been revealed (Walker 1974, 19).

It is no surprise that, with their variety and their strong element of discussion, such approaches could be made to appeal strongly to boys.

Even in the survey schools, with some exceptions, the use of such active techniques for handling texts was largely confined to English departments. However, it is plain that they are equally applicable to all subjects that require pupils to read effectively. A whole school policy for promoting either boys' achievements in particular, or literacy in general, would benefit by using them widely.

They are techniques that may also assist pupils whose basic skills are weak. However, it was far more difficult for English departments to provide direct instruction in basic skills to pupils who, usually owing to a school's limited resources, did not qualify for SEN help. In this regard, the constraints of the national curriculum and of the secondary school timetable, as well as limitations in the availability and expertise of staff, all played a part.

CASE STUDY: 11-18 comprehensive school
A Y8 Reading and Research Course

The course is offered to all Y8 pupils for one lesson per week. It was devised and is taught by the English department.

Course aims:

to support the continuing reading development of pupils by making them aware of:

- differing types of text and how they are constructed
- appropriate strategies to meet the reading task reading as a research skill and a tool of learning
- appropriate note-taking and summary methods the relationship of reading to the writing task

to foster:
- a love of reading, especially of fiction, for its own sake
- the independent learner

The course recognises the entitlement which pupils have to continuing teaching in the area of reading skills and their need to access text efficiently and sometimes independently as part of their experience of the whole curriculum.

The course will provide specific guidance on: *reading strategies*, give a variety of *reading experiences* in a supported situation, broaden pupils' *choices in fiction* and foster a *climate where the pupil interrogates the text* in order to make meaning and to learn. Over the three terms, key skills such as research reading, will be introduced and revisited in appropriate context. Homework will be used to reinforce learning where appropriate.

The broad areas for the three terms are:
Autumn Term: A Reading Programme and Study Skills
Spring Term: Text Types and DARTs
Summer Term: The World of Fiction, including analytical techniques.

In addition, reading awards (for completed fiction) are offered to students. Detailed plans have been drafted for the teaching of each lesson in the course. Next year staff from other subjects will join in its teaching.

The testing of students before and after the course suggests clearly that substantial gains in reading age have been made.

4. Explicit attention to structure

The English departments in the survey took unusual care both with the planning and presentation of their lessons. Matching their own overall organisation, they placed strong emphasis on the self-organisation of their pupils and on supporting them with adopting structured approaches to thinking, and to writing in particular. Several departments were in schools where teaching method had been the subject of school-wide priority setting.

In addition to the characteristics listed under whole school approaches (above), some key features of work in English that helped boys included:

- short structured tasks with clear targets and deadlines

- praise in public and rebuke in private

- beginning with analytical tasks, *before* discussing feelings or empathy

- storyboards and similar analytical and planning techniques adopted from media studies

- approaching literary texts from the standpoint of media studies e.g. comparing different film versions of key scenes in *Macbeth* as a way into the text

- offering media studies as an alternative option to English Literature in GCSE

- offering English Language as an alternative to English Literature at A-Level

- the frequent use of DARTs – as above

- finding plenty of room for discussion

- giving a prominent place to non-literary materials (newspapers in particular)

- offering systematic prompts to assist with re-drafting

- the use of photocopied scripts for editing exercises, both with the whole class and in groups

- a Y10 non-narrative writing assignment based on a discussion of recent national statistics for GCSE English (*and the contrasting performances of boys and girls that are revealed*)

- an English department diary for all KS3 pupils (to promote self-organisation, self-review, to monitor reading and display evidence of progress)

- planned opportunities for the use of ICT (including in one case the use of a portable suite of lap-top computers with the whole class)

- emphasising collaborative approaches to learning

- building well-conceived elements of drama into the teaching regime

- brainstorming and allied planning and discussion techniques.

In addition, several English departments had been prompted by Exeter University's EXCEL project to develop a range of new techniques and strategies for helping pupils to structure their written work. In particular, they adapted the principles of the 'Writing Frame' for a wide range of English assignments; these included both note-making and more continuous writing in a variety of non-literary genres (see under Lewis and Wray in the references below).

5. Ethos and expectations

When asked directly how they had brought about their successes with boys, two or three Heads of English found it difficult at first to answer. They saw most of the effective planning and lesson preparation that has been described above as matters of course. When pressed, they attributed their successes less to specific measures than to their general awareness of boys' attitudes, to the classroom ethos created by their teams and to the expectations of attainment, presentation and behaviour that they consistently maintained. In one of these examples, the gap between boys and girls in GCSE English (around 15 per cent nationally) had been closed to about 7 per cent in their latest results. 83 per cent of the entry had gained grades A*-C; the award of higher grades in English Literature was better still.

6. Boys' interests and preferences

Most of the effective practice described above was also underpinned by teaching materials that had been selected with an eye to boys' tastes and interests. This was seldom the chief strategy for raising boys' achievements, but was an important part of the armoury. Schools made it acceptable for boys to read non-fiction, promoted fiction with them and selected materials with a strong appeal for them. In particular, to support the sessions of planned silent reading noted above, their strategies included boys' book boxes and thematic and genre-related book collections (e.g. horror, science-fiction, X-files analogues and fantasy, myth, and teen-age problem stories); collections of books by Terry Pratchett were especially popular. English departments and school librarians worked together to ensure that boys' interests were met in both their sets of collections. In addition, to support the voluntary reading of pupils with special needs and of underachieving readers in general, collections of attractive books of low readability were placed on open shelves in the library; no stigma appeared to be attached to their use.

However, many heads of department were dismayed by the change of direction in set-book selection for GCSE that has followed recent adjustments to the National Curriculum for English. They noted that what they judged to be an increased emphasis on pre-twentieth century literature had been particularly prejudicial for boys of below average achievements and motivation.

7. Groupings

Two schools had experimented with single-sex classes for English and several of the other heads of department were emphatic concerning the principles underlying their own grouping systems. Across the sample, entirely opposing principles were adopted, but the schools found that what they had attempted appeared to work effectively.

Both the single sex pilots had tried the system with one year group; each felt sufficiently encouraged to carry the pilot forward for at least one more year. On a point of logistics, both felt that they could not have embarked on their experiments so readily had the numbers of boys and girls not been nearly equal in their chosen year groups. Both schools set pupils by ability in English. Both also consulted parents before beginning their pilots. They monitored pupils' responses closely, but it will be some time before they can be certain of their outcomes in terms of achievements in national tests or public examinations. After one year, both schools now plan to modify their arrangements: they will broaden the ability range of their upper sets in particular. In one case, after polling the pupils' preferences, top sets will revert to a mixed sex grouping while middle and lower sets will retain their single sex organisation. The school notes that the year of single sex teaching had improved the achievements of abler boys enabling them to join mixed top sets in more equal numbers with girls.

Contrasting mixed ability and mixed sex groupings were used with equal success. In one school where mixed ability teaching is used, mixed gender seating arrangements are emphasised in English as a matter of explicit policy. It is a school where GCSE English results are well above the national average and the gap between boys' and girls' achievements much narrower than the national picture.

The survey evidence does not resolve the arguments for or against single or mixed gender grouping arrangements. The conviction with which a particular form of organisation is used appears to be much more important.

Conclusions

This survey suggests that there is no magic bullet, no quick measures that take immediate effect with boys' literacy. However, it also carries a number of firm and positive messages: in particular, the survey schools took clear measures to address a problem and they made a difference.

One of the clearest *whole school messages* must be that carefully conceived policies to identify and target underachievement can also work well for boys' literacy. Policies directed towards an overall raising of literacy levels can be similarly effective; they usually benefit boys in particular. An enhanced awareness of the needs of boys is equally important; it is especially effective where it is reflected in the daily practices of subject departments. Measures specifically directed towards boys' interests and preferences can also be helpful, but they are less likely to be adequate in the absence of more overarching policies concerned, for example, with teaching quality across the school.

When he enters the secondary school, the boy with poor basic literacy is acutely disadvantaged. First he must catch up and then he must keep up. But the National Curriculum is a set of moving targets: it makes new demands on his first day and proceeds on a steep upward curve. Two messages were especially clear to the *special needs teams* in the survey schools:

- *Rapid progress with basic literacy is essential in the secondary school.* It is likely to require intensive teaching early in Key Stage 3.

- Using a variety of strategies, the skills that the poor reader is taught need *well co-ordinated reinforcement*. In particular, the skills need to be practised. And progress needs to be prompted and praised in a partnership between home and school.

English departments are concerned with the whole ability range. The most effective were clear in their objectives, explicit in their emphasis on teaching and practising the skills of literacy and tightly organised in the classroom. In particular, they were teams that were aware of the needs of boys and had established an ethos of high and consistent expectations. They had adopted a developmental and self-monitoring approach to their work.

Two schools were moving towards policies that involved *all departments* in taking explicit and practical daily account of the particular kinds of literacy demanded by their own subjects. It is a logical extension of what is described in this paper. In combination with what has already been noted, it holds out the prospect of further significant gains for boys and girls alike.

Beyond the control of the individual department are *overarching matters* of the organisation and resources needed to enhance the literacy of boys. Setting arrangements for one department should not determine those for another subject; splitting classes between two or more teachers is unhelpful to continuity, especially for weak groups; and effective withdrawal arrangements for intensive literacy teaching need the strong support of the senior management team. Where resources hinder the SEN team from addressing all but the severest cases, secondary school English departments that attempt to teach the skills specified for Key Stages 1 and 2 are likely to experience difficulties with timetabling, with staff expertise and with materials. In addition, as OFSTED has recently reported, 'poor provision of books adversely affects standards' in one in six English departments (OFSTED 1997, 5).

Participating schools

Acklam Grange School, Lodore Grove, Middlesborough, TS5 8BP.

Alcester High School, Gerard Road, Alcester, Warwickshire, B49 6QQ.

Archbishop Ilsley RC High School, Victoria Road, Birmingham, B27 7XY.

Arrow Vale High School, Greensward Lane, Redditch, B98 0EN.

Arthur Mellows Village College, Helpston Road, Glinton, Peterborough, PE6 7JX.

Arthur Terry School, Kittoe Road, Sutton Coldfield, Birmingham, B74 4RZ.

Ash Green School, Ash Green Lane, Coventry, Warwickshire, CV7 9AH.

Chantry High School, Martley, Worcester, WR6 6QA.

Henry Beaufort School, East Woodhay Road, Harestock, Winchester, Hampshire, SO22 6JI.

King James School, St Helen's Gate, Almondbury, Huddersfield, HD4 6SG.

Lings School, Billing Brook Road, Northampton, NN3 4NH.

Newsome High School, Castle Avenue, Huddersfield, HD4 6JN.

Sackville School, Lewes Road, East Grinstead, West Sussex, RH19 3TY.

St Benedict's RC High School, Alcester, Warwickshire, B49 6PX

References

Basic Skills Agency (1994): *Basic Skills in Prisons: Assessing the Need.* London, The Basic Skills Agency.

Bynner J and Parsons S (1997): *It Doesn't Get Any Better: The Impact of Poor Basic Skills on the Lives of 37 Year Olds.* London, The Basic Skills Agency.

Clay M M (1991): *Becoming Literate: The Construction of Inner Control.* Auckland, Heinemann.

HMSO (1993): *The Gender Divide: Performance Differences Between Boys and Girls.* London, HMSO.

Lewis M and Wray D (1996): *Writing Frames.* Reading, Reading and Language Information Centre (University of Reading).

Lunzer E and Gardner K (Eds.) (1979): *The Effective Use of Reading.* London, Heinemann Educational.

Lunzer E and Gardner K et al. (1984). *Learning from the Written Word.* Edinburgh, Oliver and Boyd.

Manguel A (1996): *A History of Reading.* London, Flamingo.

OFSTED (1993): *Boys and English.* London, OFSTED.

OFSTED (1995): *Guidance on the Inspection of Secondary Schools.* London, HMSO.

OFSTED (1997): *Standards in English.* London, OFSTED.

Plackett E (1995): *Developing a Whole School Approach to Reading in the Secondary School.* London, Borough of Lewisham, Education Department.

Sylva K and Hurry J (1995): *The Effectiveness of Reading Recovery and Phonological Training for Children with Reading Problems.* London, SCAA.

Walker C (1974): *Reading Development and Extension.* London, Ward Lock Educational.

Wray D and Lewis M (1997): *Extending Literacy: Reading and Writing Non-Fiction.* London, Routledge/Hutchinson.

5

Raising boys' achievement in English

How an action research approach had a major impact on boys' literacy at the Wakeman School in Shrewsbury

Val Penny

Back in April 1993 I was appointed as Head of English at the Wakeman School in Shrewsbury. It was at this time that the Adviser for English, Peter Traves, distributed a paper summarising the key findings of the 1993 OFSTED report, *Boys and English*, which had been published recently. This chapter describes how research helped my department to tackle issues concerning boys' underachievement.

The results of interviews with samples of students and questionnaires on attitudes to English provided the basis for developments in classroom practice and specific initiatives in approaches to teaching and learning within the department. Increasingly, curriculum development focused on improving boys' standard of performance and literacy through innovative approaches to the English curriculum, particularly non-fiction reading and writing.

Responses to the Boys and English report

The Wakeman School English Department was strong on principle and keen to improve, but there was some reluctance to get involved in any project that involved only boys. Although our boys were not under-achieving in relation to national standards, we did agree that our girls were achieving better results in English than our boys were. We therefore agreed that the present level of underachievement should be tackled as a matter of some urgency.

As a department we began to ask the following questions:

- How far are the negative aspects featured in the *Boys and English* report reflected in our practice?

- Is there a relationship between gender, potential and achievement?

- How do we, as English teachers, try to ensure that male potential is being realised as well as the potential of our female students?

- What special strategies can be adopted in the classroom to improve the performance of boys?

Project Planning

We felt that the issue of raising boys' achievement ought to be set in the wider context of raising achievement for *all* students by continuing to provide a rich and varied English curriculum. A long-term plan of action research with students as key participants was decided on – we felt that it would have a major impact on classroom practice because specific research findings could be applied immediately. We trusted that our students would be able to provide us with valuable information about their learning experiences, which would help to identify specific strengths and weaknesses. Whilst this feedback would assist us in targeting specific issues, it also placed pupils at the centre of their learning.

Before we started our research we decided that:

- We should remember that it was not only boys that were under-achieving.

- What applied to some of our boys also applied to some of our girls.

- Strategies that addressed the underachievement of either gender should focus on good teaching practice.

- Nothing we did to raise the achievement in English should be to the detriment of either gender.

- A focus on good teaching practice would be of benefit to all of our pupils, those that were underachieving and those that were not.

- We should remember that all schools have different agendas and needs; therefore, what might be successful in another school, might not work for us.

We decided to interview stratified random samples of students about their experiences of the English curriculum and to use questionnaires developed by ourselves with whole year groups.

Phase 1 results

In September 1994, a development group of Shropshire Heads of English, interested in raising the achievement of boys, was set up under the auspices of Shropshire RAISE. The first phase of our development plan was thus supported by RAISE funding and the work of the Boys and English Group led by Ann Malcolm, Advisory Teacher for English.

Year 9 Questionnaires

After a department meeting focusing on the issues raised in *Boys and English* and in the department action plan resulting from our February 1994 OFSTED inspection, it was decided that we would focus our attention on the issue of reading. We were particularly concerned at the dip in library use by Year 9 students and the whole department felt that the present Year 9 would benefit from increased support for their independent reading, research and library skills.

The project took the following form:

- baseline questionnaire

- results analysed and supporting strategies to be put in place

- feedback from Advisory Teacher and boys in English group

- interviews with a small sample of students

- evaluation of supporting strategies.

All students in Year 9 completed our questionnaire and the findings from this study were discussed with English staff. A sample of the results is featured below (boys' results are the solid black, girls the grey):

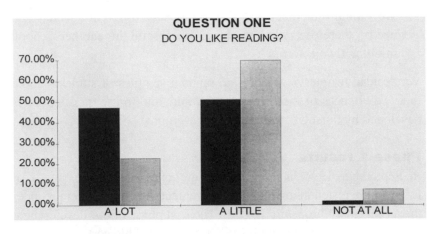

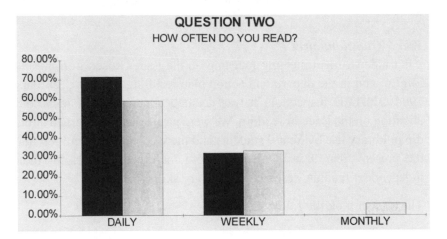

One outstanding feature of the initial results has been the marked difference between boys' and girls' reading networks and the more positive commitment to reading from girls.

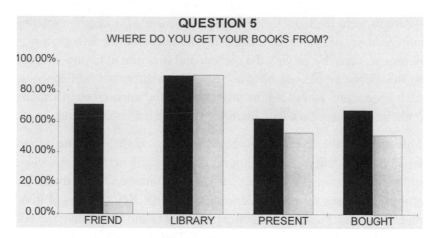

QUESTION 5
WHERE DO YOU GET YOUR BOOKS FROM?

Clearly, there was a need to increase the frequency of library use by boys and to provide opportunities for them to share their reading preferences with others. After much discussion, the following recommendations were made:

- To evaluate existing library stock to ascertain whether it meets our pupils' needs

- To introduce a reading journal for all pupils so that greater interaction took place between student and teacher

- To monitor pupil journals and teachers' responses

- To introduce an extra independent reading session of 30 minutes

- To share good practice in supporting reading in Year 9

- To evaluate future library use by Year 9.

As a result of this investigation, a number of developments took place. For example, library sessions were broken down to shorter sequences of different reading activities. More varied reading tasks, short-term reading targets and more opportunities to discuss reading preferences were introduced. These measures improved both the amount of reading tackled by Year 9 and the quality of the reading materials tackled. Successful reading activities were shared between members of the department and greater emphasis placed on the concept of reading as a 'diet' which would include non-fiction, poetry, biography as well as fiction.

Attempts were made to tackle the development of a negative reading culture in several ways: by increasing the range of drama activities in library sessions; by varying the content and structure of library sessions so that pupils would not be able to predict what would be happening each lesson; and by raising the awareness of the importance of reading non-fiction in those readers, mainly girls, who read only fiction.

This phase of the research into boys' attitudes, highlighted the importance of providing a challenging range of reading activities and close individual support, so that readers were encouraged to set their own ambitious targets for their independent reading. Key features of good practice in supporting and encouraging readers and in the planning and organisation of lessons were identified. This study also suggests that there is a clear link between good teaching and the development of committed readers and that the good teaching of reading is particularly important for boys.

Key elements that led to its success are as follows:

- Talking about reading and sharing reading experiences helps to counteract the more negative attitudes towards reading

- Talking about reading supports boys because it helps to give them the confidence to try new genres and tackle more demanding texts

- A formal presentation of research findings can help to make boys more positive about their reading because such an activity raises the status of non-fiction texts

- Working with a reading partner (or partners) particularly benefits boys

- Boys enjoy more practical investigations in reading, particularly role-play, because they work best when they are actively engaged in their work.

Year 9 interviews
Initially we targeted our year nine pupils because they were at the end of Key Stage 3 and might therefore be able to offer us a wide perspective of their experience. Interviews were conducted with six groups of pupils, four single sex groups and two mixed groups.

The main findings were:

- All pupils wanted even wider experiences of drama and all valued oral work most highly

- Both sexes enjoyed active approaches to Shakespeare

- Students were most positive about drama, ICT activities (not only word-processing), working in various groups and theme based units such as Holiday and Theme Park

- Girls preferred sustained reading activities, whereas boys wanted reading time broken up

- Boys needed more support and encouragement in supporting their choice of reading material. They enjoyed media and ICT texts more than girls

- Both sexes, boys more so, wanted to study far more contemporary fiction including film and other media texts

- Both sexes enjoyed expressing their views in written and spoken argument. Boys were less positive about justifying opinions and using evidence to support their views

- Both sexes preferred the opportunities of written coursework rather than time-constrained assignments. Boys, however, preferred their work to be marked in several sections so that they could revise their plans as they crafted the final written essay, rather than on completion of a complete draft

- Both sexes, boys more so, were positive about creative writing and poetry.

Year 10 questionnaires

Year 10 students responded to a questionnaire that focused on attitudes to English. They were asked to respond in some detail to specific prompts. General findings indicated that boys:

- Preferred a more active learning style

- Enjoyed working in groups, including mixed ability and mixed gender groupings

- Enjoyed drama

- Enjoyed opportunities to express their opinion

- Valued non-literary texts, including film

- Preferred to have a choice of assignments or have the opportunity to negotiate aspects of the assignment

- Preferred their work to be responded to by oral feedback in a one-to-one situation or written feedback that was both specific in detail and supportive in tone

- Preferred regular homework and teacher intervention

- Recognised the importance of external examinations.

We also examined attitudes to types of text and teaching and learning styles.

The way forward

The results of interviews with samples of students and questionnaires on attitudes to English provided the basis for developments in classroom practice and specific initiatives in approaches to teaching and learning within the department. Our professional development days were used to develop fresh approaches to the curriculum.

As a result:

- Greater opportunities to use active approaches to the English curriculum, especially oral work, were included in new coursework units

- It was decided that each major coursework assignment would include target setting, so those students were more clearly receiving the information they needed on how to improve the quality of their work

- The curriculum in Year 9 was modified to include timetabled use of the drama studio specifically to support the use of active approaches to the study of *Romeo and Juliet*

- A greater emphasis on consulting pupils led to increased knowledge about pupil perceptions of our setting arrangements.

In conclusion, feedback from the first round of pupil interviews and questionnaire research helped the development of the English curriculum, including developments in pupil groupings and oral work.

Pupil groupings

In response to the concerns raised during the interviews, the issue of pupil groupings both within the year group and in the classroom was studied over a period of four years. The results of the initial investigation clearly revealed the predominance of girls in the upper ability sets, an imbalance in curriculum provision and a gap in examination performance at GCSE.

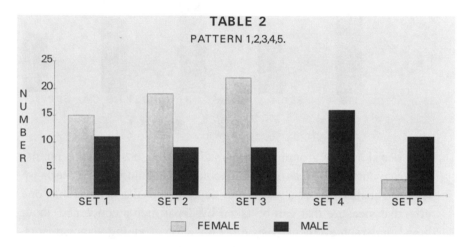

TABLE 2
PATTERN 1,2,3,4,5.

The figures shown in Table 2 support the OFSTED findings:

> *In almost all the schools there were more girls than boys in the upper ability groups and more boys than girls in the lowest and this may be a factor contributing to boys' poorer performance in English. The general absence of clearly thought-out and well-defined criteria in placing pupils in different groups suggests that the degree of differentiation may owe as much to teachers' expectations as to contrasts in boys' and girls' abilities in English.* (OFSTED 1993)

We felt that the criteria for the sets had never been clearly defined and that students were being grouped according perceived ability. Therefore, we drew up an extensive list of ability indicators across the three assessment areas, which we decided to use for grouping pupils in future. In compiling these indicators of potential, we focused particularly on how members of the department recognised indications of underachievement and potential. This led to more grouping using broader bands of ability, as can be seen in Table 4.

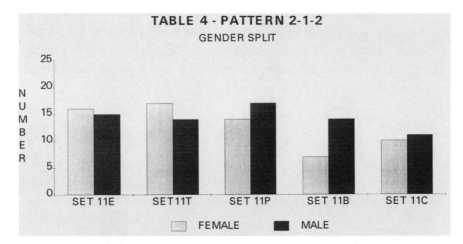

TABLE 4 - PATTERN 2-1-2
GENDER SPLIT

Our decisions on grouping were made on the basis of the pupils' achievements in all areas of the curriculum, according to the criteria we had established for use within the department. We believe that one effective measure that can be taken by departments concerned about boys' underachievement is such a review of grouping arrangements, both across the year and within the classroom. We believe that every pupil should be grouped according to his or her potential, rather than performance in an internal examination, SAT or her/his achievement in written work. The criteria for grouping or setting should also be made available to all parents.

Single sex subject mentoring

'Enhancement' was a mentoring scheme for our C/D borderline candidates. Although this opportunity was given to both sexes, it was principally taken up by boys who wanted to achieve a grade C pass in English and English Literature. In addition to mentoring exclusively for English, pupils were mentored as part of the school scheme. Scrutiny of examination results indicated the scheme was successful. Levels of confidence, the ambition to succeed and examination results were improved in the target group. The results of this work were reported in March 1996 in the OFSTED/DFEE Publication, *Setting Targets to Raise Standards: A Survey of Good Practice*. Our work is featured as Case Study No 10.

Increasing the amount and quality of oral work

Why did we decide to focus on oral work when we had set out to tackle the underachievement of boys?

- We felt that oracy was the first stage of literacy and that better managed oral work could be a way of extending boys' language range and power

- We needed to build on boys' enthusiasm for and strength in oral work by helping them to develop more sophisticated skills. Boys are more likely to feel that they have a 'stake' in the lesson when their preferred style of learning is a focus of the lesson. This, in turn, would affect their attitude and behaviour

- Increasing the frequency of oral work was recognised as a key factor in improving the performance of girls in science and mathematics. Therefore, we believed that it would lead to more active pupil involvement in lessons

- We needed to begin with the positive and focus on what boys are better at. The existing assessment focus tended to be on the aspects of English that girls were good at.

Emphasis was placed in our development plans on raising the status of oral work because we believed that, by developing oracy, we would also enhance our pupils' literacy. Increasing the variety and quality of oral work would lead to more variety in the structure of lessons and in teaching and learning styles. We found that this helped to address the problems of those pupils with a shorter concentration span. Seating resources were controlled in order to maximise control and minimise off-task behaviour. We wanted to improve learning attitudes because they minimise the time spent off-task and the time spent by the teacher in dealing with other interruptions that detract from the quality of teaching and learning in the classroom.

Pupils were introduced to mixed gender groupings and became familiar with working in different groups, of varying sizes, for different purposes and units of work. They were encouraged to work in mixed-gender pairs or in small groups. We found it important to vary the grouping – pairs, fours, mixed ability groupings. Well-managed oral work also provided opportunities for boys to develop an awareness of their own strengths and weaknesses in specific types of talk and in specific situations.

We wanted particularly to offer support for more formal styles of speaking and our development plan included an increased emphasis on public speaking. Our students entered the Mock Parliament competition, the Bar Council's Mock Trial Competition and *The Observer* Mace Debating Competition, and they also appeared in Chester Crown Court. These outside competitions provided opportunities for the study of the language of debate and the language of the courtroom. They also helped to provide the impetus for the development of new schemes of work for GCSE oral work.

Classes enjoyed writing their own ground rules for good oral work. This helped to address some of the issues about boys' weaknesses in oral work, whilst at the same time, ensuring that girls contributed to oral work more effectively. It also helped to ensure that boys listened more closely and reflected on their contribution and that girls had the maximum opportunity to offer and support ideas and to take on leadership roles.

Phase 2 Research

After evaluating the success of our Phase One research, we looked again at introducing classroom strategies we felt might be useful. One strategy we introduced to support boys' achievement, and which we feel is effective, is called 'Home and Away'. Seating management has helped to improve pupil behaviour and this involves pupils working a particular assignment in 'home' (managed friendship groups) and 'away' (mixed ability and mixed gender groups) for particular lessons and activities. Both 'home' and 'away' groupings are changed at a minimum of once a term, so that pupils have the opportunity of working at least once in an academic year with every student in their teaching group.

'Home and Away' groupings help to ensure that cliques do not develop and that unhelpful pairings can be dealt with in a positive way. It also ensures that in the teaching of the lesson, most emphasis is given to the majority, those that are doing well. We have found that a seating and group work plan helps the teacher to target those pupils who need more teacher support and intervention.

We also wanted to review:

• the scheme of work for Key Stage 3

• the department's marking policy to give greater consideration to student feedback, both orally and in writing

• the suggestion from our students concerning the marking of longer pieces of coursework in sections.

Introducing new schemes of work to support boys' learning

We have also introduced more demanding oral work lower down the school. For example, a unit entitled 'Persuasion', for our Year 9 pupils, explored human rights issues and included opportunities for students to analyse the techniques of persuasion in a range of speeches and to deliver their own. Pupils, including those with statements of special educational needs, made speeches in assemblies and in a formal pre-sentation to their peers, which was recorded on video. It was noticeable that some pupils – girls as well as boys – produced their best work of the year in this unit.

In an end-of-year self-assessment one boy wrote: *'I am proud of a lot of my work. The main good points are my speeches on the street children of Guatemala and my speech criticising teachers.'* One girl commented: *'I have always wanted other pupils to listen to what I really have to say, and now they have!'*

Important factors that we feel contributed to the success of this unit were:

• As we were then a totally female department, the use of an outside male speaker (the chairperson of the local Amnesty International group) to start the project off and later to be part of the audience for their final speeches. The use of male role models is an area we intend to develop in the future, particularly in a project that involves pupil research in surveying what materials, especially books, that men read

- The strong response of the pupils to the study of contemporary issues on human rights. We also wanted pupils to see that men could take on the caring and affective role

- The focus on the variety of technical skills needed in a successful speech as well as on the content and the structure of an argument.

The Ambassador Project

In 1996-7, we won financial support from the Centre for the Study of Comprehensive Schools, under the Education Industry Partnership Award Scheme, for a special project. The theme was 'Education for Citizenship', with the focus on raising the peer group status of a group of pupils (both boys and girls) whom we felt were underachieving. The project gave them the opportunity to realise, and indeed make others realise, that oral skills have an increasingly important and vital role to play in the world outside school. The Ambassador Scheme also gave our students opportunities to practise their oral skills in a variety of realistic settings.

The department's marking policy

From our research, we found that students valued our positive feedback. We now offer more detailed advice than we did previously and we ensure more specific praise. However, we realise that boys generally prefer specific praise for written work to be given quietly and privately, whereas general praise, especially for oral work, can be given more publicly. Students use comments by their teachers as an aid to personal target setting. This is why our comments aim to help pupils identify what they need to target next and what techniques they should be developing to improve their level of achievement.

At GCSE level, every teacher spends considerable time in giving one-to-one support. We want to help students to 'unpick' their targets, overcome their barriers to success and thus make more rapid progress. We also introduced more regular opportunities for self-assessment because we believed that students valued opportunities to reflect on their successes in English and on their progress in the subject. It has enhanced student motivation and their understanding of what they had to do to improve, even though we have found that the 'unpicking' stage requires more individualised support than we had previously thought.

Phase 3 Research

As a result of the Phase 1 and 2 research findings, we decided that we should look more closely at the attitudes of boys and girls on entry to the Wakeman School. We found marked differences in their feelings about the subject:

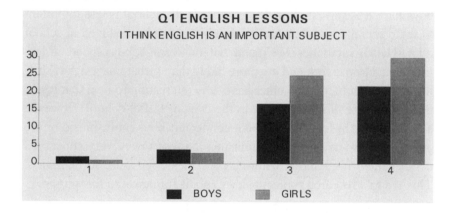

Attitudes towards teachers were also different:

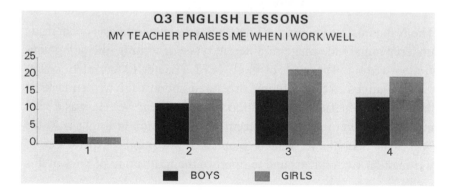

National research into attitudes and habits related to school, particularly that of Keele University, reveals similar tendencies and trends: boys have less 'invested' in schools than girls; school is less important to them socially and they are less likely to become involved in school related leisure activities. We found that, on average, boys spend far less time doing homework and are more likely than girls to have a part-time job out of school. On the other hand, it is interesting to note that it was girls who were going out most in the evenings after school. However, almost all of these activities were connected with sport, music or the guides. Follow-up interviews indicated that boys were very concerned about handwriting and structuring their ideas, far more so than girls. This led to a research project using explicit frameworks for writing.

Using writing frames to improve boys' writing

Boys' preferences were on the whole for factual and informative writing. (OFSTED, 1993)

The National Curriculum for English has a clear emphasis on students undertaking a wide range of different types of writing, including non-fiction writing. The work of the EXCEL (Exeter Extended Literacy) project suggested that offering structured support for written tasks is particularly beneficial to boys. Success in writing, we felt, was a vital ingredient in improving self-esteem and motivation in English. At the Wakeman School, we wanted to enhance our pupils' experiences of writing non-fiction texts and to improve the motivation of boys in this subject.

The work of EXCEL and the book *Writing Frames – Scaffolding Children's Non-Fiction Writing in a Range of Genres* (Scholastic Books, 1996) by Maureen Lewis and David Wray (of the EXCEL project) were important aids to our planned curriculum development. Children do not need help only with the planning and structuring of their writing, but also with the linguistic devices that help hold the text together. As Lewis and Wray maintained, 'The frames in this book are starting points which teachers can develop for their own unique classroom contexts and purposes' and that is just what we decided to do.

The Writing Frames Project – Phase 1

As pupils progress through school they are expected increasingly to be able to use more sophisticated writing forms, including the discursive style. In our work with pupils, we wanted to help them improve their discursive writing and, in particular, to move beyond a simple 'for' and 'against' model of argument to one demanding a more sophisticated evaluation and synthesis of evidence. The weighing of arguments, supported by evidence, is the traditional academic style, a style with which few of our pupils were familiar.

To support them, we decided to use the EXIT model proposed by Lewis and Wray that identifies three important stages of progression:

• teacher modelling

• joint activity

• independent activity

We first used writing frames to teach non-fiction writing in a unit of work written for Key Stage 3 students. The unit invited pupils to investigate the question '*Do UFOs really exist and have they visited Earth?*' by evaluating evidence offered in media and other non-fiction texts, including CD-ROMs. In addition to teaching discursive writing skills, we wanted to improve pupils' reading skills and, in particular, their ability to challenge the reliability of their sources. The unit focused on the use of media and non-fiction texts and included opportunities to use both spoken and written argument forms.

The project involved the use of a clear plan of action which set out to detail the writing and reading skills needed and exact order and development of classroom activities. The investigation began with the study of a newspaper article and a video about the Roswell Incident, which were the focus of the teacher-led activities that supported stage one of the Lewis and Wray model. DARTS reading activities were used in the initial stages of the investigation to model the reading and note-taking skills that pupils would need in the later stages of the project.

Groups of pupils were then given the task of collecting and evaluating additional evidence to support the investigation. They collected their evidence from a range of sources including CD-ROMs, magazines and videos, using the skills they had learned in the more teacher-directed activities in the shared text. Considerable in-class support was given through a display board crammed with information at various levels of complexity and three or four videos available for smaller groups to view.

Records were kept of the articles read and there was an emphasis on annotating any photocopied textual information with questions to establish the reliability of the evidence. (We knew from our previous research into boys' attitudes to English that more use of modern media would enhance their learning but, in practice, we found girls equally keen to tackle this topic.)

This stage of the investigation was undertaken in mixed gender and mixed ability 'away' groups. Each member of a group of four (a 'home' group) was given a particular focus for research. They then joined members of other home groups, making an 'away' group. Each 'away' group was given the task of investigating one of four topics: alleged abductions by aliens, reported sightings of UFOs; the truth about Area 51 or how NASA has tried to reach other life forms. The results of these studies could then be fed back to the home group, thus reducing the amount of research that needed to be tackled by any one student. (A full report of this unit of work may be found in *Raising Boys' Achievement in English*, published by Shropshire LEA.)

We found that the most-able students used the frame as a springboard for their ideas, whilst those who were less secure in writing in this style found the level of support very satisfying. Another important support for these weaker students, many of whom were boys, were the steps we took to build up their confidence in using this more formal type of language through oral work.

This project engendered a more positive attitude to English, especially amongst boys – not only the *will* to do well but also the *skill* to do well. The reasons for this were:

- The nature of the task complemented the interests of the teaching group

- The task involved contemporary non-fiction magazine texts and video recordings

- We provided opportunities for children to select information

- We provided a structure for the written task

- The writing frame helped pupils with the language links they needed to transform their planned argument into a piece of coherent prose

- We provided opportunities for them to experiment with language structures.

This investigation supported our view that students can tackle demanding texts and written tasks if they have a clear understanding of the nature of the task. When the task is broken down into smaller steps and 'unpicked', pupils were able to work more independently and to a far higher standard. One pupil with a statement of special learning needs wrote the most extended and complex essay he had ever written and was able to discuss his ideas confidently and offer evidence to support his views. All boys were more successful in tackling this topic, but girls were even more so. They seemed to 'munch' their way through the framework material with a real appetite for the writing freedom it gave them.

The Writing Frames Project – Phase 2
After both pupils and staff had judged the initial project a resounding success, our interests turned to Year 10. The focus group was a class of thirty students who were banded into an 'upper' group. There was a considerable range of ability and confidence in using a more formal language in the written form. The idea of using the writing frame

approach in secondary schools had been explored in an article by Elizabeth Plackett (*English and Media*, No.35 Autumn 1996), but no mention had been made of working at Key Stage 4.

One additional feature of the Year10 investigation was the development of a concept ladder. The purpose of the concept ladder was to assist pupils in modelling their writing more independently, whilst also revising some of the key issues of the work studied in class. The concept ladder was a group of statements that pupils had to examine in pairs. If they agreed with the statement, then they needed to find evidence for their views in their research. The concept ladder aimed to push the class into planning their own, tightly organised, assignments. Pupils were also encouraged to underline and highlight key areas of the texts that they would need to refer to at a later moment in the drafting stage.

Writing frames and concept ladders worked extremely well with boys, especially those who were less secure about their language skills and those who normally lacked confidence in their planning. Students enjoyed the opportunity of being supported whilst at the same time maintaining their independence as learners. Girls, however, completed work of an even higher standard than the boys and they used the frameworks and the concept ladders in a more imaginative and sophisticated way, almost as a springboard to a higher level of competence.

Extract From A Concept Ladder – Media Unit
ENGLISH DEPARTMENT
Planning Ladder
MEDIA ASSIGNMENT

- This activity will help you plan the content of your essay and help you to begin to collect specific evidence to support your views. You can use these phrases just like a writing frame.

- Working in pairs, read the following statements and decide which ones you think are true and which are false.

- Look at your list now and think how you might justify your decisions. Look for specific evidence from the newspaper articles we have studied or other work we have done in class. Use specific quotations from the media texts to back up your views. Write your ideas down on paper for future reference.

- Look at your notes again. Are there any statements you agreed with that might contradict one another? Do any of these ideas link with one another? Number them to help you in your planning.

- *The words 'newspaper **story**' are accurate.*

- *There are fundamental differences between broadsheets and tabloids in terms of layout, content, tone and style.*

- *Newspapers would be uninteresting without some scandal.*

- *The front pages of tabloids are far more lively and colourful than that of broadsheets.*

- *Newspapers guide our views of society.*

- *Broadsheets cater for a more literate reader who wants to be informed, not entertained.*

- *The camera never lies.*

- *Tabloids place their emphasis on human interest stories, rather than actual current events and foreign news.*

Out of the teaching group of thirty, a sample of fifteen was taken to ascertain pupil perceptions of the research and to discover how the concept ladder or writing frame had helped students to make progress in their reading and writing. Pupils were simply asked to make a free comment on lined paper about the project – anonymously. The most frequently recorded comments are tabulated below:

CONCEPT LADDER COMMENTS	FREQUENCY
Extends my understanding of the material.	9
The statements help me think for myself more.	11
They point me in the right direction for planning.	8
They help me to work out what quotations I shall use.	7
WRITING FRAME COMMENTS	**FREQUENCY**
Makes my vocabulary more mature.	10
Helps me to start sentences.	6
Helps me to link ideas.	7
Gives me the confidence to write complex sentences.	6
Gives me a clearer structure for the language.	9
Widens my vocabulary.	7

The final evaluation of the discursive initiatives indicated the following:

- A well-planned scheme of work, including opportunities to practice research techniques, was essential

- Opportunities for students (especially boys) to hear transcriptions, or read scripts, of discursive pieces written by their peers helped pupils to become aware of the features of good technique

- Mixed group activities and whole class and group discussions helped pupils to develop the cases for and against (especially the synthesis charts)

- Writing frames proved to be useful in supporting pupils' writing in the drafting stages because they helped pupils both to organise their ideas and to express and link them more effectively

- The discursive frame needed adapting for each assignment and for pupils of different abilities

- Boys enjoyed the role-play activities, practical aspects of the investigation, the use of information technology and audio-visual aids. Because these were used, the boys said they felt better motivated and they felt that they achieved greater success

- Almost every pupil achieved a standard of work that was well above his or her previous level of achievement.

In Year 10, this work has been built upon in three consecutive assignments and the standard of assignment produced each time has been higher. It was interesting to note that, under the pressure of 'mock' examinations, this group of students used the writing frame phrases to organise their written responses more effectively.

Boys and English – four years on

Four years on from the start of our work focusing on boys' achievement, current initiatives in our department include the following:

- A continuing focus on the encouragement of an independent reading habit in Year 7, through to Year 11

- New units of discursive writing for our students

- As a direct result of the success of using a writing frame with KS3 students, a group of most able students were involved in similarly successful work

- Information Technology is increasingly being used to underpin good practice in the English Department and the number of pupils attending our ICT club has grown by over 50 per cent. We regard our increasing use of ICT in English as a response to the changing nature of literacy. It is part of our commitment to finding the necessary resources to support a pupil's entitlement that will include the use of electronic texts to enhance the teaching and learning opportunities provided by more traditional resources

- Department development has reflected the evaluation of the research already completed and INSET has been targeted accordingly.

An evaluation

The measures described in this case study have raised the level of boys' achievement. They have not, however, substantially reduced the gap between boys' and girls' achievement because, inevitably, girls also benefited by the changes we introduced. The continuing existence of this gap might seem initially disappointing, but it has always been a fundamental principle of the Shropshire RAISE Boys and English project, and of the Wakeman School English Department, that nothing done to raise the achievement of boys should be at the expense of girls. We realise that raising the achievement of boys closer to that of girls, in terms of 'hard' results at GCSE level, is a long-term goal, which needs to be considered in the context of value-added information.

Steps taken to enhance student learning have included:

- A focus on more active learning opportunities in the English curriculum, especially to give pupils the skills to control their own words and ideas and to gain independence

- More emphasis on the variety in teaching and learning styles

- A greater emphasis on the use of real audiences for pupils' work. More effective use of target setting. This includes helping pupils to 'unpick' the steps needed in order to accomplish longer-term goals

- A greater emphasis on consulting pupils. Feedback from the pupil interviews has helped the development of the English curriculum, including changes in the way we set homework

- A greater emphasis on the importance of speaking and listening, including public speaking

- A continuing emphasis on raising the profile of reading. This is through a focus on private and group reading, collaborative book reviews, the use of CD-ROMs, book weeks and visiting authors

- A continuing emphasis on good practice in recognising and supporting pupil achievement through the use of positive marking and the setting of realistic short term and longer term targets with students.

In our drive for the continuous improvement of standards in our subject, what is interesting is that all of the steps that have been undertaken to improve the performance of boys, have also improved the performance of girls. Our research shows that good English teaching is important for boys and girls, but especially so for boys. The evidence from the research is that students recognise which approaches to teaching and learning are most successful and can describe how teachers can bring out the best in their abilities.

Indicators of these improvements are that:

- Pupil self-review indicates that our students, especially boys, have received the new curriculum units very positively

- There are now fewer discipline problems with boys within the department

- There are now fewer problems with regard to the completion of homework and coursework assignments

- There is less off-task behaviour by boys

- There is a marked improvement in the self-esteem, attitude and rate of progress of less able male students.

- There has been a very positive response to the changes in grouping

- Male and female students are using ICT more frequently in their English assignments outside of lesson time

- The presentation of English GCSE coursework and Lower School assignments has been vastly improved.

Boys also gained motivation from taking a more active role in their learning and acting as co-researchers. This proved to be a powerful tool in the department's strategy of raising the achievement of boys.

We have found that investigating student attitudes to work in English is vital to an English Department's effectiveness. Three main points have emerged:

- Students welcome the opportunity to be consulted about the development of their curriculum and this has a positive effect on their attitude to the subject

- Sometimes the findings challenge stereotyped views of boys' and girls' attitudes

- Knowledge of a teaching group's attitudes to English and information about the aspects of the curriculum that they find most difficult, or indeed enjoyable, plays an essential part in the planning process for differentiation in the classroom.

In conclusion we believe that in tackling the underachievement of boys in English, we need to remember that schools can make, and do make, a difference. While being aware of the broader issues, we need at individual, departmental and school level to focus on where we can have an impact, whether that be on the ethos and attitudes, on helping teachers and children, on the school and subject curriculum or on teaching and learning styles. However, there is no magic quick fix solution! The issues are complex and therefore effective strategies may take several years to impact. 'Hard' evidence, in the form of changing patterns in exam results, may take several years to emerge.

Nothing done to enhance boys' achievements must be at the expense of girls. Valid ways of tackling *all* underachievement are likely to impact on the achievements of both boys and girls. In our desire to tackle the underachievement of boys, we must not neglect the teaching and learning needs of our girls. Girls need a positive view of themselves as learners, just as boys do. Both sexes need to know that their achievements are appreciated as this makes such a positive base for future progress.

Finally, involving pupils in school development is now seen as a critical issue in the raising of achievement in schools, particularly that of boys. School self-evaluation can be carried out through interviews with specific groups within schools. If we want to enable students to talk about their progress and how the curriculum can be improved to match their needs more closely, then one task included in a school's curriculum for oral work should be a problem-solving task – helping the English Department to improve!

6

A multi-layered approach to raising boys' (and girls') achievement at the Vale of Ancholme School, 1993-1996

Brian and Liz Terry

Introduction

The Vale of Ancholme School is an 11-18, mixed comprehensive in the new Unitary Authority of North Lincolnshire. It has some 620 pupils on roll who largely come from five village primary schools in the area around the small market town of Brigg. Vale is also a centre for Special Educational Need, with some 5 per cent of the pupils having statements for a wide variety of physical and learning needs. It has a policy of integrating all SEN pupils into mainstream education. In 1992, Vale and its partner primary schools began work on a joint Equality of Opportunity policy, under the leadership of Mary Meredith as Equal Opportunities Co-ordinator and with the support of one of the joint authors of this chapter, Liz Terry, as Headteacher. The other, Brian Terry, was involved in a consultancy role from the outset and was able to pursue it more actively when appointed as Curriculum Development Initiative Co-ordinator for the Scunthorpe Area of Humberside from

September, 1993. (The CDI was the Humberside Technical Vocational Educational Initiative (TVEI) Project and had Raising Achievement and Equality of Opportunity as two of its agreed aims. The Scunthorpe Area became North Lincolnshire following local government re-organisation in April 1996.) A cross-phase initiative was inherited which was unique in Humberside and enabled a more comprehensive approach to raising achievement.

An analysis of GCSE results showed marked gender differences with girls outperforming boys in a number of curriculum areas. The girls' performance was also very close to that of boys in subjects, such as Mathematics and Science, which were traditionally seen as 'boy friendly'. This very much reflected the national trends but was exaggerated in English, with 28% of boys, compared with 64% of girls, achieving a grade C or above at GCSE. A survey of pupil attitudes to schoolwork and subjects was carried out in all the partner schools early in the autumn term of 1993. This showed that pupils had quite clear perceptions of their strengths and weaknesses before arriving at the secondary school. Boys' and girls' attitudes to language-based work started to diverge around Year 5. The poor perception of boys towards their language work and their measured ability declined relative to that of girls as they got older. The poor attitude found in the primary schools to more language-based subjects mirrored the under-achievement of boys at GCSE.

Defining the issues

The work on attitudes to language clearly suggested one path to take in tackling this issue, i.e. raising boys' performance in language alongside raising achievement for all pupils. The school was already using the TVEI Project to support a review of teaching and learning styles, and the introduction of more effective differentiation based on the work promoted by Rob Powell. Another consultant, Geoff Hannan, had been used by the school to launch the Equality of Opportunity policy development, so his support and advice were sought to highlight the changes in classroom practice required cross-phase to build the balance of skills needed by both boys and girls to succeed.

The Vale of Ancholme School was committed to achieving Investors in People (IIP) status and was using a programme from The Pacific Institute called Investment in Excellence (IIE) as a vehicle towards IIP. IIE is a powerful personal and institutional development programme that was devised by Lou Tice, founder of The Pacific Institute. It was soon clear that this also had much to offer pupils, particularly where self-esteem issues are a bar to achievement. This then defined the second strand of the work, i.e. adapting and using IIE related materials to raise the self-esteem of pupils.

The final issue to be addressed, in essence, grew out of the monitoring of results that started the work in the first instance. There was a clear need to be able to analyse the general progress of pupils and the gender/ achievement link in more detail. This would help identify existing good practice and enable the school to track progress towards the narrowing of the gender divide. It also provided a tool in itself, in that it gave progress data for individual pupils which could be used to inform the target-setting negotiations as part of the assessment, recording and reporting process. There was an intention from the outset of this work to extend it to partner primary schools, again emphasising the cross-phase nature of this work.

Thus, by the end of 1993-94 there were three clear areas of work aimed at raising achievement in general, and that of boys in particular:

- improving differentiation and changing classroom practice

- building self esteem

- monitoring pupil progress and target setting.

The funding of this work came from a variety of sources: TVEI School and Consortium budgets, School GEST (Grant for Educational Support and Training) budget, and Humberside TEC (Training and Enterprise Council) through their partnership initiative to raise achievement in schools. The use of funding will be dealt with further as each strand of the work is expanded.

Happiness goals an underlying principle

'Children who behave badly in school are those whose self esteem is threatened by failure. They see academic work as 'unwinnable'. They soon realise that the way to avoid losing in such a competition is not to enter it.' Elton Report (1989, 106)

People are teleological in nature: we are all goal, or end-result, orientated. We embark upon a task because of what we think it will give us as a reward at the end. Schools work, by and large, because the pupils adopt the goals presented by each school as their goals. The rewards that the school offers become the pupils' rewards. These can vary from short-term rewards, such as the praise of peers, parents or teacher, to gaining a major recognition, in terms of a certificate of achievement, or good grades in external examinations. Overlaid on the institutional goals are those that the children bring with them. In a rural comprehensive, social and friendship goals are of particular importance when it may be difficult to meet outside the school environment because of transport difficulties. Certainly, those pupils who have no 'happiness goals' to achieve by coming to school often become school refusers.

Good education is, by its very nature, challenging in that it is trying to move the child forward from the current level of learning to a new level. When faced with a challenging target, this creates in us a tension that gives us the energy, and switches on our natural creativity, to reach the target. Pupils with a good self-image as a learner will take on the task, but those who think that they cannot achieve the target will take all their energy and creativity to avoid doing the task. This 'creative avoidance' operates largely on a subconscious level, but often affects their own learning and that of others. Creative avoidance is often characterised by pupils starting to misbehave, wanting to go to the toilet, wanting to talk to the teacher or someone else, becoming very helpful in order to waste time, and displaying a whole range of other behaviours to avoid the task in hand and, thus, avoid failure.

It seems that more boys in our schools opt out of the academic race through fear of failure. We see more boys in lower sets, more boys being statemented, and more boys being excluded from schools. Once the opt-out process starts, it can become a self-fulfilling prophecy, producing even lower levels of self-esteem as a learner. Since we have given girls access to the whole curriculum and told them that it is for them, through such initiatives as Women into Science and Engineering (WISE) and TVEI, they seem to have developed a virtuous self-talk cycle promoting even greater achievement. We must get more boys to enter the 'race' and to think that they can win in it.

Changing classroom practice: differentiation

Rob Powell was engaged by the Scunthorpe and Grimsby TVEI Consortia to deliver a number of workshops for all curriculum areas covering the issue of differentiation. This work was funded from Consortium budgets, but attracted support from Humberside TEC and County TVEI funds. The authors had already heard Rob Powell and Chris Dickinson talk at a one-day conference and, recognising the relevance of the content, the staff at Vale were given a one-day training session led by Rob. Following this launch, individual staff were able to opt into the workshops in order to give them more time to develop the ideas into practical actions. The core of the work was to explore in depth the range of available strategies covering differentiation by *content, task, resource, support, outcome* and *response*. The promotion of 'study guides' to make clear the learning targets for pupils, coupled with the setting of individual targets for improvement, made it easier for the pupils to line up their personal goals with the 'big picture' of teaching goals. The nature of the differentiation process gives pupils greater access to the 'academic race' with an increased chance of being a 'winner'.

Changing classroom practice: gender issues

Geoff Hannan, as previously stated, had already worked with the Vale staff and pupils as part of the launch of the Equality of Opportunity policy development process. He was engaged to work with the secondary school and all partner primary schools to deal directly with the gender issues. Geoff delivered a series of workshops for pupils at all levels during the spring term of 1994. The workshops highlighted the changes in classroom practice that he advocates in order to raise achievement for all pupils by using compensatory practices to suit the differing learning needs of boys and girls. The pupil sessions were linked to staff development meetings in the schools involved.

In terms of understanding this work, it is important to consider the 'learning cycle' and some of the key ideas that lead to our understanding of the 'truth' about the world, as we see it, and how this 'truth' is passed on in the education process. The learning cycle can be summarised as follows:

As soon as we are born, we start to build up our view of how the world works. This gives us a picture of what is natural.

↓

We then seek out those facts that support our view of what is natural. This gives us a picture of our world as 'factually correct'.

↓

This 'factually correct' view of the world contains our 'truth' and value system, which we use to guide our everyday actions, and makes us 'blind' to issues around us.

↓

As friends, parents, teachers, managers etc. we do what is expedient, guided by our value system and world view.

↓

We may then, unthinkingly, give out messages, sanctions, or do those things that are discriminatory or harmful to others.

↓

Thus, we create a social environment from which the next generation will build its view of what is natural.

Fifty per cent of what is natural in our view of how the world works is in place by the time we are four: a further 30 per cent is in place by age eight (Dryden and Voss 1994, 223). Much of our children's gender-based behaviour that affects learning is already forming by the time they reach primary school. It is well entrenched by the start of secondary education. Thus, it is important to intervene *early* in the education process, and this very much supports the key place of the cross-phase work in the project.

Before we intervene, however, we must start to understand what it is we imprint on our boys and girls and how this affects their preferred learning styles. This is not the place to explore the nature verses nurture argument, but suffice it to say that we must give some credit to both genetics and nurture in the development of the individual.

Boy and girl babies are treated and handled differently from birth (Blackman *et al* 1987, 48). These differences in treatment are subconscious on the part of adults and are based on their view of what is both 'natural' and 'factually correct'. The language used about girl babies reflects the view that they are made of 'sugar and spice, and all things nice'. Girl babies are talked to more than boy babies, encouraged to smile more and, on the whole, large arm movements elicit soothing behaviour from adults. Little girls are encouraged to be quieter and less adventurous, with tears being seen by adults as a sign of fear. Boy babies are talked to, and expected to behave like the 'slugs and snails, and puppy dogs' tails' that make them up. Crying is more often seen as a sign of anger and the boy is expected to be both noisier and more adventurous than a girl. Parents handle boys more, stimulate them more, and large arm movements are likely to get the parent to encourage outgoing and exploratory behaviour.

This stereotyping continues with clothes, images from greetings cards, types of toys, and expectations about forms of play. There is also a tendency in parents in general, and fathers in particular, to be intolerant of what they perceive as cross-gender behaviour, with fathers showing least acceptance of 'feminine' behaviour in their sons. The child's view of what is 'natural' will then be related to gender with boys knowing, in particular, that they must on no account be like girls.

Girls learn that they should be:

• quiet and passive

- better communicators and able to use more reflective forms of language

- able to play co-operatively with others.

Boys, conversely, develop:

- competitive natures

- good risk-taking skills

- better spatial awareness and understanding of objects and systems.

When a child enters formal education, skills of working quietly and getting on well with others are valued. Certainly, in classes, conflict resolution by fighting is discouraged! Girls have the learning skills that give them a head start in classroom behaviour. Their superior language development – especially in reflective use of language – gives girls an advantage in literacy work. As education then progresses, the ability to express oneself through the written form becomes increasingly important, with much formal assessment being through written outcomes. Boys are less prepared for the education process in general, and for the development of literacy in particular. Many of them then feel that language-based work is not their forte, with the consequences we see and experience in our schools.

Geoff Hannan proposed three practical classroom strategies to balance the skills of boys and girls: structuring classroom talk, using the language hierarchy, and group work.

Strategy:	For girls:	For boys:
Structuring classroom talk	Add risk-taking	Add language
Using language hierarchy	Add speculative use of language	Add reflective use of language
Group work	Add objects and systems	Emphasise relationships

Structuring classroom talk

This focuses on developing risk-taking skills in girls, while at the same time improving boys' use of language. Geoff Hannan advocates abandoning the use of hands going up at the start of lessons as it encourages the more confident pupils, with up to seven boys' hands going up to one girl's. The teacher then goes to the boys and, in the authors' experience and observation, often gets an ill-considered response. The preferred strategy is to ask a question of the whole class with a clearly defined expectation as to number of responses and a set time. Pupils then talk and work out a number of possible responses. Individuals are asked to respond by name. Girls can safely risk an answer, having gone through their preferred learning style of language use. Boys will have gone through a language process before being allowed to risk an answer. All pupils, therefore, will be actively involved in the education process from the start of the lesson.

It is important to affirm the desired change in classroom behaviour. Children must be given approval by the teacher for the language/risk-taking process, even when the answer they offer is wrong. Without such affirmations, the pupils have nothing to gain from the behaviour change. A correct response should get an unconditional affirmation, such as: *'That's right. Thank you for that'*. An incorrect answer might be countered with a conditional affirmation that divides the response from the action of risk-taking, such as: *'Thank you for your answer. I'm not sure about that. What do you think?'* This last question is addressed to another pupil, with the teacher returning to the original pupil to make sure that (s)he has understood and affirming that understanding.

It was the experience of many of the teachers in the project that this form of questioning can be applied at any appropriate point in a lesson. Insisting on full sentence responses, which can be of particular use where children speak a language other than English at home, can extend it. If a sentence is given incorrectly, the child can be asked to repeat the corrected sentence and that correction affirmed.

Using the language hierarchy

Geoff Hannan's second strategy involved the idea that language is a hierarchy that goes *descriptive, reflective* and *speculative.* This leads to effective language flow in lessons. He asserts that when the hierarchy is absent, there is less effective use of language and learning itself is reduced. Boys need the language to be structured to lead them from descriptive levels on to reflective use of language where they have a weakness. Girls are good at both descriptive and reflective language use, but need support in moving to speculative levels. This flow from descriptive, through reflective, to speculative should be part of each section of work. The authors, and other teachers involved in the project, also found that written work benefits from reflecting this hierarchy: it must be considered in designing worksheets, written/assessment tasks and choosing textbooks. A typical example of using the language hierarchy might be as follows:

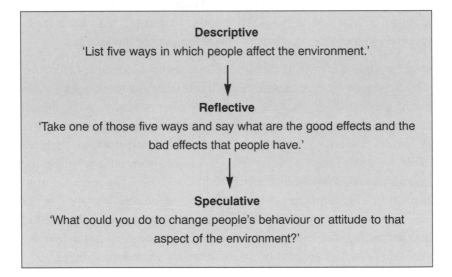

Group work

Geoff Hannan's final strategy for the schools to adopt was related to group work. He advocated a pluralistic approach to group work: *single sex friendship groups, single sex non-friendship groups* and *mixed gender groups*. Mixed gender groups encourage boys to develop better language skills from girls (particularly the reflective use of language), while girls are helped to move on to the speculative level. Girls are able to use objects and systems better without boys and they may be able to risk-take more safely at times in single sex groups. It was suggested that learning activities take place in pairs or groups for 50 per cent of the time. In line with the similar advice from Rob Powell, activities were to be structured carefully and have regular time checks built in. A clear target was to get each child to work with every other child in the class at least once during the school year. Geoff Hannan's preferred target is for all children to work together during each term.

Single sex friendship groups help pupils to:

- learn how to help each other
- learn how to co-operate and share tasks
- address gender stereotyping and reduce inhibitions
- improve their communication skills.

Single sex non-friendship groups help pupils to:

- learn how to compromise and co-operate with others
- become more outgoing and responsive to others
- broaden their views and become more tolerant of the views of others
- understand that you do not have to be friends to work together productively
- improve communications skills.

Mixed gender groups help pupils to:

- learn that boys and girls can contribute equally and differently to the same task
- develop their interpersonal skills and have respect for the opposite sex
- improve their communications skills
- avoid distractions and urges to 'show off' in mixed company
- compensate for weaknesses and increase their range of preferred learning styles.

As with other changes in behaviour, it is important to recognise and find ways to affirm the success of pupils in different groupings and activities. *Appendix 1* shows how the English Department at Vale incorporated these changes in practice into a policy document.

Raising self-esteem

As part of its drive for the Investors in People Award, Vale of Ancholme School used the Investment in Excellence programme from The Pacific Institute for all staff during 1994 and 1995. This involved a considerable financial investment on the part of the school, not least because the IIE course lasts five days. After introducing the programme to key staff using Humberside-run courses during working days, the bulk of the staff were trained by using residential weekends at a local hotel. This avoided the cost of supply teachers and the inevitable disruption to pupils' education, while providing a comfortable environment for participants. The success of the course for staff can be measured by its attractiveness, even at weekends, such that the vast majority attended the programme. It also led to the school being awarded the Investor in People standard in February 1996.

Staff who had gone through the IIE process wanted to give elements of the work to the pupils at the school. A working group of interested staff from local schools was established during the summer term of 1995, funded jointly by TVEI and Humberside TEC, to explore the adaptation of materials for secondary pupils. The Pacific Institute already had a booklet-based product which could be adapted from 'American' to suit an English audience of Year 7 or 8 pupils, called 'It Starts with Me!'

Work of this nature had already been done at William Gee School in Hull. William Gee was ahead of Vale and the Scunthorpe Area because it had completed the IIE process a year earlier. Unfortunately, it is an all-boys school, which meant that its adaptation of 'It Starts with Me!' showed largely male images. The Scunthorpe working group then had the job of balancing the gender images and refining the excellent work undertaken under the leadership of Georgiana Sale, Deputy Headteacher at William Gee. The Pacific Institute must be thanked for allowing us the freedom to adapt and use its copyright material.

The modified workbook for pupils was completed ready for trials to start at four schools during 1995-96. Each school had opted to use the booklets in either tutor-led or timetabled PSE with either Year 7 or Year

8. A questionnaire was given to all pupils at the start of the programme that gave a measure of self-esteem. This was repeated at the end in order to note any changes. Pupil interviews were also used after the programme to gauge reaction (see *Appendix 2* for extracts from the evaluation produced for Humberside TEC).

At Vale the programme was delivered to Year 8. A full day was given over to the launch of 'It Starts with Me!' at the beginning of the autumn term. It was then delivered in a 30 minute extended tutor period once a week. The full programme took two terms to deliver. The pupils were happy to keep on with the work, but the staff consensus was that it was too long!

Key features of the booklets were:

• they were produced to a high standard, with covers customised for each school

• pupils were able to make the booklets their own by adding photographs and drawings

• pupils had control of the work they did in the booklets

• they were confidential to each individual and they showed to other people only those things that they wished them to see.

Essentially, the programme got the young people to examine where they were in their lives, the positive and negative sides to themselves and what influenced them. From this, they were able to understand the importance of self-talk and how to build a virtuous self-talk cycle. They learnt to understand the influences, both negative and positive, that they had on those around them and how important it is to give both self, and others, positive feedback. They were shown how to analyse negative comments rather than to take them as automatic 'truth' about themselves. They could then choose to ignore unhelpful comments, and accept feedback constructively. Finally, some thought was given to how each person might wish to change his or her self, what prevents us changing ourselves, and the use of affirmations as a way of bringing about lasting change. The use of personal affirmations is a key to change: affirmations from outside the individual may help the process of improving self-esteem, but only the individual can sanction and bring about changes in self.

The participation of nearly all the staff (including non-teaching staff) in the IIE process made it easier for the school to adopt a range of affirmation strategies for all the pupils:

- smiles, nods, 'well done' etc. as simple unconditional affirmations

- more formal, unconditional affirmations, such as notes in planners for parents to see, putting work on display, etc.

- conditional affirmations of the form shown below, which were less effective than unconditional affirmations, e.g. *'keep up this standard of work and I can see you doing well'* or *'when you get on with your work, your results are really good'*

- praising a child's work to a visitor to the classroom or sending them to someone they see as important for praise, e.g. to have some work displayed in the Headteacher's office

- using awards and certificates as affirmations of success and giving them due weight.

Many of these strategies were already in place as part of the rewards structure within the school, but IIE reinforced their importance and enabled staff to be more positive in their attitude to pupils. This is important when research indicates that 'most children, from a very early age, receive at least six negative comments to every one of positive encouragement.'(Dryden and Vos, 1994, 229).

Boys who suffer from low self-esteem as learners are likely to harass and bully those who wish to do well. It is common for boys not to be able to show interest in class or complete homework effectively because of taunts. Pupils with high self-esteem can resist these taunts and are unlikely to engage in such name-calling themselves. The Vale had a clear behaviour code. Where behaviour fell outside the code, there were clear sanctions. The issue of concern was separated from the individual so that it was clear that the behaviour was condemned, not the person. As educators, we can just as easily reinforce a negative self-image as a positive one.

Monitoring pupil progress and target setting

Kenn Todd, the deputy with curriculum responsibility at Vale, worked with Mary Meredith to produce the initial gender analysis that was the starting point for this work. He wanted to be able to see the potential for each pupil and, ultimately, give each one a value-added profile. The data would also be used to highlight successful curriculum areas and pinpoint good practice on the part of individual teachers.

CAT (Cognitive Abilities Test) scores from Year 7 and Year 9 were initially used to define the potential of children. The whole school assessment policy was reviewed to give a high level of consistency to the ability grades given to each pupil on a half termly basis. A programme to record and analyse the data was developed based on Excel, with TVEI and TEC funding. This was part of a consortium activity involving five secondary schools, but clearly led by Kenn Todd as the prime mover. Teachers put their data directly into the programme using networked computers based in the staffrooms and using a scale that gave a simple numerical score linking National Curriculum levels to GCSE grades.

Analysis of the data not only gave a snapshot of how the individual pupil was progressing, but showed where there were problems. Information could be framed in terms of a comparison with a variety of other pupils: all pupils of similar ability, all pupils of same gender, etc. The information could then be fed into the review of overall progress carried out by tutors. This enabled discussion with pupils to start from a more objective standpoint. From this review, more realistic targets for raising achievement could be set, which could then be entered into the newly designed pupil planner. The data is being further refined by the addition of Key Stage 2 and 3 test results. Kenn Todd is also working to extend the process into partner primary schools.

Summary

The full value added system was introduced during 1996-97 and will need time to prove itself, as will all the other initiatives. In the short term, the school has made progress in raising the achievement of all. The 1997 GCSE results with value added data are as set out below:

5+ A*-C GCSE	Boys	Girls	All
Potential	27.4%	38.5%	32.5%
Actual	29.0%	42.0%	35.0%
Value added	+1.6%	+3.5%	+2.5%

These results belong to the Year Group at Vale that had the workshop with Geoff Hannan as Year 8, and his strategies applied from September 1994. The year group which will have all the strategies applied will be examined in 1999. Only time will tell if the gender gap closes alongside raising the achievement of all the pupils.

Acknowledgements

Geoff Hannan Training, Bank Cottage, Bourton Road, Much Wenlock, Shropshire TF13 6AJ (01952 727332)

Network Educational Press Ltd, P.O. Box 635, Stafford ST16 1BF (01785 225515)

The Pacific Institute, 145 Kensington Church Street, London W8 7LP (0171 7279837)

References

Blackman S, Chisholme L, Gordon T and Holland J (1987): *Hidden Messages, The Girls and Occupational Choice Project*. Oxford, Basil Blackwell.

DES (1989): *Discipline in Schools* (The Elton Report). London, HMSO.

Dryden G and Vos J (1994): *The Learning Revolution*. Aylesbury, Accelerated Learning Systems Ltd.

Appendix 1
Strategies to Improve Use of English
English Department Policy, September 1994

Vale of Ancholme School

Groupings

* As far as possible, balance the gender of groups.

* Impose a seating plan so that there are not whole male or female sections in classes. Change this periodically.

* Direct small-group activities so that, where appropriate, there are mixed groups. Girls learn risk-taking; boys develop language skills.

* Do not allow groups to self-select.

Activities/Lesson Content

* Use 'active questioning' to encourage boys to reflect, i.e. question followed by 1/2/3-minute paired discussion – or note taking – followed by teacher selecting B/G/B/G to answer.

* Structure talk around the language hierarchy – descriptive, reflective, speculative – so that there is natural progression and language flows.

* *'Well managed oral work improves boys' attitude to English and their performance.'* Make this central. Provide opportunities, before writing, for pupils to talk their way through to understanding.

* Provide 'real purposes' and foster a sense of audience in oral and written work.

* Make the subject more 'boy friendly' by exploiting boys' interest in the relationship between people and things. Use I.T., for example.

* Encourage, monitor and guide reading by checking 'Reading Records' regularly and make suggestions.

* Avoid reinforcing stereotypically insensitive masculine identities through unduly sharp critical comments on work.

Appendix 2
Extracts from evaluation of 'It Starts with Me!' programme in North Lincolnshire as they apply to Y8 pupils at Vale of Ancholme School

Quantitative evaluation

Pupils completed the pre- and post-programme questionnaires. The results show a greater improvement for girls compared to boys. Boys improved by 11.1%, girls by 22.7% and pupils overall by 16.4%.

Qualitative evaluation

Six pupils from each tutor group were interviewed. The pupils were selected by the school to be representative of the year group in terms of gender and ability. The same broad range of questions was put to all groups in 20-minute interviews.

• Two thirds of pupils took the booklets home to work on them.

• Where parents had seen or talked about the programme with their children, there was a positive response. The school received no formal comments, positive or negative, from parents.

• Two thirds of the pupils thought that the programme had made a clear and positive change to their self-talk. Of the others, about half felt that they were already positive, e.g. 'Helped me improve my marks on tests' and 'I'm not embarrassed when I am good at something'.

• About one third of the pupils said that the programme had improved their relationships with other people, e.g. 'I treat my mum better now' and 'Me and my sister used to argue all the time but we've settled down now'.

• Two thirds of the pupils said that they would continue to use the booklets at home to add compliments and to use when feeling low.

• There was an almost unanimous view that the programme should be repeated and that they would like extension work in future years. It was the best part of the year's PSE programme.

7

A different style of learning
The route to raising boys' achievement at Notley High School, Braintree

Alan Davison and Christopher Edwards

1992 marked the 21st birthday of Notley High School in Braintree, Essex. Celebrations were muted, as there seemed little reason to have a party. The school had just lost its sixth form in a county reorganisation. The roll was falling, in part due to demographic changes, but also because the school was losing more able pupils to rivals with a greater reputation for academic success. The lack of examination success at Notley could be seen starkly in the new and controversial examination performance league tables. The 29% 5+ A-C rate had been an improvement on the previous year, and brought the school in line with the two other schools in the town. The league table position, however, looked decidedly unimpressive when compared to the schools in nearby small towns, which now had the added advantage of offering 11-18 education.

The need was to raise academic achievement; *the challenge was to overcome the view held by staff at all levels that the current achievement was a fair reflection of the pupils' potential.* The processes developed to identify and tackle underachievement were not initially designed to focus on gender differences. In 1992, boys' relative per-formance to girls was not the national issue it has become. The school's need was to raise achievement by boys and girls. Only later, when the techniques adopted had produced significant improvements, did it become apparent that as achievement increased across the school, the boys were being left behind.

The importance of performance data

Throughout the period 1992-1995, a number of techniques were developed and refined to identify and measure relative underachieve-ment. The first approach was to analyse GCSE results to identify achievement in each subject relative to:

- the same pupils' overall achievement
- national performance in that subject
- previous years performance.

Such data was given a very high profile in the school with all staff and governors in order to create a culture that said raising examination achievement was the main priority. It included subject 'league tables' recording pupils' average GCSE point scores in the subject against the scores achieved in all their GCSEs. Underachieving subjects had no hiding place: their performance was open to public scrutiny. The improvement in the 5+ A-C percentage rate from 29% to 47% in two years indicated that something was working in terms of establishing an 'achievement culture'.

Clearly, a school can bring about a certain degree of improvement by putting achievement in the spotlight. The prospect of falling rolls leading to redundancy, combined with the improved morale arising from the initial successes, created a strong impetus in staff. There was a limit, however, to how much further improvement could be achieved without a more sophisticated approach. The arrival of a new head in 1993 gave the work a fresh direction. What was now seen to be as important was to identify underachievement in Years 9 and 10, so that *potential* underachievement could be addressed. The problem was what data existed that could be used to identify whether a pupil was perform-ing to his or her ability. The obvious approach was to try to use some prior achievement data and relate it to current or predicted achievement.

NFER (DE) scores were readily available, based on tests undertaken in the feeder primaries, although up to this point the data had been put to little use in school, outside of the Learning Support Department. For Year 10, the scores were compared to GCSE grade predictions made in the spring term. Various methods were tried to present this information. The one that staff found most accessible were scatter graphs with trend lines (see *Figure 1*).

Figure 1

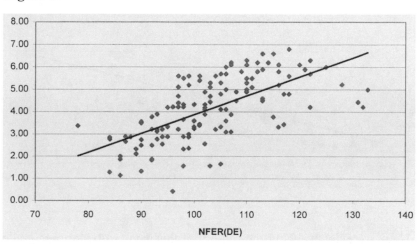

The average GCSE grade was plotted against the NFER score and a trend line inserted. The points below the line indicated pupils doing less well than the average for their peers, while those above the line are doing better. All points within one GCSE grade of the line were considered to be insignificant. The pupils whose points were outside the margin were identified and targeted for extra support. The system was easy to operate and the information caught the imagination of staff. The graphical representation of the data brought home the message that students of similar potential ability were achieving at widely different levels, but more significantly the tabulated data upon which it was based provided a wealth of information for different teachers to use.

Such was the usefulness of this technique that a means to provide similar information on Years 7-9 was considered essential. Initially, attempts were made to replicate the process using National Curriculum levels. These were found to be undiscriminating, as in a typical Year 7 or 8 over half the cohort were assessed at the same level. The performance data that was chosen was an average of the norm-referenced achievement grades on annual reports. These grades were plotted on a scatter graph against their NFER (DE) score, as before. An example is shown in *Figure 2*.

Figure 2

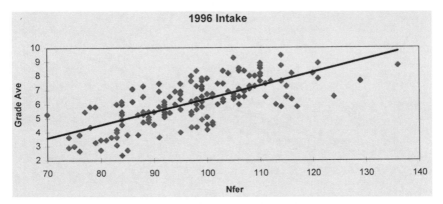

There were doubts about the validity of this data, as the average grade scores seemed a crude measure of achievement. The precaution of building in a margin of error by discounting scores close to the line was used again. The approach had none of the credibility that national value added systems carried, but at least the information was immediate. Staff could look at the performance data of students within two weeks of the assessments. The genuine sense of interest and excitement the data produced was characterised by the impatience to receive the data in days, rather than weeks. If nothing else, the technique was getting a large number of staff to focus on the performance of individual students.

Although this approach had not set out to focus on gender differences, the staff easily recognised a consistent pattern in the data for every year group. *The majority of names below the line were boys, those above the line, girls.* In 1995, attention to this issue was seen as a priority. The year group who would be sitting their GCSEs in the summer of 1996 was a demographically 'freak' year of 101 boys and only 52 girls. The school would be unable to sustain the improvement in its exam results that had contributed so much to raising its profile and morale unless it could do something about boys' achievement in particular.

The theoretical basis

Having identified a problem, the school began the search for a practical solution. A team of teachers and advisory staff from the LEA examined the research base. Several areas proved compelling and relevant to our situation.

The medical evidence suggested that boys have a reduced capacity for verbal reasoning and analytical skills, with girls being more sensitive to sound and able to detect intonation patterns at an earlier stage (Arnold 1997). This reflected our experience of boys arriving at the school with poorly developed language and reading skills. Our primary feeder schools had perceived a similar problem. There are attitudinal differences between boys and girls toward schooling. Boys often seek refuge in a counter-culture that allows them to maintain their self-respect, which is all-important in their peer relationships (Downes 1994; Warrington and Younger, 1996; Wheatley, 1996).

Boys have an over-confidence in their own ability and a willingness to blame others, particularly teachers, for their failure (Balding 1994; Licht and Dweck 1987). This corresponded with the classroom experience of the teachers involved and matched with the results of our Keele University Pupil Perception Data. One reality we could not evidence from the research base, but wonder whether this may ring true to readers, is the number of able boys who remained as 'one of the lads' whilst working hard and securing the top GCSE grades in the school.

Michael Barber stated that, in his view, literacy is the most important factor:

> *We know that in reading boys already trail girls at the age of 7. The gap has widened by 11. Those who arrive at secondary school with inadequate reading competence are predominately, but of course not solely, boys. Their inadequacy in this respect prevents steady progress and can lead them into lack of motivation, disaffection and sometimes truancy.* (in Bray et al. 1997)

This confirmed our empirical evidence established through an examination of the pupils' reading ages, Key Stage 2 results and the difficulty boys were having accessing texts in the classroom. Further empirical research also highlighted the significant difference between boys and girls involvement in reading for pleasure.

A senior colleague attended a seminar run by Geoff Hannan and was strongly influenced by his ideas on the different preferred learning styles of boys and girls, e.g.

> *He has a trial and error, experiential learning style rooted in confidence, competence and interest in the manipulation of objects and systems: a speculative thinker... She has a language-centred, sequential learning style, rooted in an interest in people and relationships: a reflective thinker.* (in Bray *et al*. 1997)

It was this thinking which influenced our approach to raising boys' achievement. Hannan stressed the need to recognise the difference between boys' and girls' approaches to the same given task.

Raising Staff Awareness

The clear message from the research work was that to have any impact on the achievement of boys, the techniques employed by individual teachers in each of their classrooms had to be changed. The approach taken to raise staff awareness had to have a direct effect on classroom practice and so a high-profile strategy was planned.

The first stage was to introduce the staff to the ideas through a two-day staff development programme. The senior colleague who had attended the Geoff Hannan seminar presented a summary of his ideas. The reasons for different preferred learning styles were explained, as it was vital that staff understood that in teaching boys and girls they were teaching people with very different needs. All teachers accept that pupils of different abilities require different teaching approaches. Staff had to be taken to a position of recognising that differentiating for gender was as valid as for ability. Accepting such a view is difficult because for so long schools have been influenced by an equal opportunities culture that seemed to deny gender differences. Evaluation of the training programme showed that the majority of staff had reached the point of acceptance. When asked what in the presentation had the biggest influence on their thinking, three different elements emerged.

For some it was the examples taken from Hannan of the different approaches to play demonstrated by young children. As one faculty head commented:

> *The description of a young boy playing actively with a car or doll using sounds not words, compared with the girl playing with the same toys but giving them names and talking to them, struck me as so true about my own children. I realised that in bringing up my own children, I had always adjusted to their different needs as a boy and a girl, but in my classroom I had been blind to the differences.*

For others, it was the more scientific explanation of nature and nurture differences, particularly differences in brain development and the ways peer pressure influence boys and girls. For most, it was the examples of gender difference they could relate to personally.

> *I think what clinched it for me was the example of how men and women tackle putting together a piece of self assembly furniture. I could see myself as the man who just starts throwing it together, getting increasingly frustrated until my wife retrieves the instructions from the bin and we start getting somewhere.*

Having gained acceptance of the need for different approaches, the training then emphasised practical classroom techniques, such as mixed-gender groupings, writing templates and approaches to questioning. To persuade staff that such approaches could make a difference, one teacher had been asked to trial the techniques with some Year 10 classes. The examples of the very positive effects they had on pupils who the staff knew by name and reputation, though anecdotal, were useful in giving other staff the confidence to try them.

The outcome of the training days was for each subject team to identify one approach they would develop collaboratively within their subject. Their work was to be supported by local authority advisors as action research projects that would be disseminated across the county.

Our Approach

Once we had successfully raised the awareness of the staff we commenced work on a number of strategies which were seen as the most appropriate for the subject content of a secondary school. The key components of our approach were:

1. The use of templates

In both English and Science, we had identified the significant difficulties encountered by the majority of boys in recording data or any lengthy pieces of writing. To assist boys with this problem, templates were designed in both areas to give clear guidance on what should be in each section of the written work.

In Science, this involved a structure that could be employed in the writing up of investigations and experiments. An example is set out in *Appendix 1*. The template provided a series of questions that guided the pupils through the process and ensured they recorded the information in sufficient detail and asked themselves the right questions. This resulted in significantly more detailed write-ups by the boys and was welcomed by them as it provided a structure for their work.

In English, the template focused on the structuring of extended pieces of writing. *Figure 3* shows an example used with younger pupils of what an essay should look like. This emphasizes blocks of writing on the same topic and paragraph indentation. It also highlights that paragraphs can be of different lengths. Paragraph 3 and 4 show examples of content guides that assist pupils in the selection of appropriate ideas.

Use of the template shows pupils what an essay looks like. It emphasises blocks of writing on the same topic and paragraph indentation. It also shows paragraphs can be of different lengths. An essay like this would be spread over 2-3 sides of a workbook. The content of the paragraphs can also be written in each block once a list of central ideas has been written on the board.

Figure 4 shows three different styles of templates for use within Key Stage 4 to assist with comparative essays on two novels. Pupils can consider which of the templates is likely to gain the best grade in GCSE coursework. The most able quickly identify C as the desirable outcome and can plan accordingly. Weaker pupils should aim for B as an improvement on A.

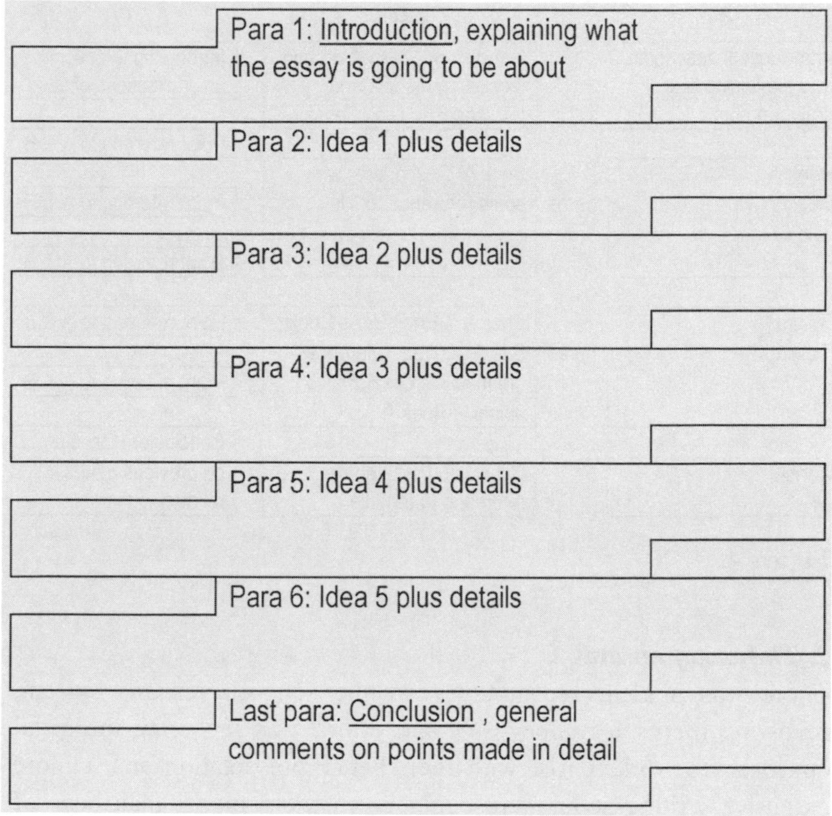

| Para 1: <u>Introduction</u>, explaining what the essay is going to be about |
| Para 2: Idea 1 plus details |
| Para 3: Idea 2 plus details |
| Para 4: Idea 3 plus details |
| Para 5: Idea 4 plus details |
| Para 6: Idea 5 plus details |
| Last para: <u>Conclusion</u> , general comments on points made in detail |

Figure 3

The use of templates proved very effective in extending the written work of boys and helping focus their work on the appropriate content. The idea is now being extended into other curriculum areas as all the pupils found the guidance very helpful.

Awareness raising was undertaken with the English Department to highlight the strengths many boys displayed in answering questions in a concise style, which often did not get the credit it deserved. We recognised a clear tendency, often denied by teachers, to reward neat, extended work that may not answer the question as accurately. This led us to look at the whole issue of what was rewarded within the school.

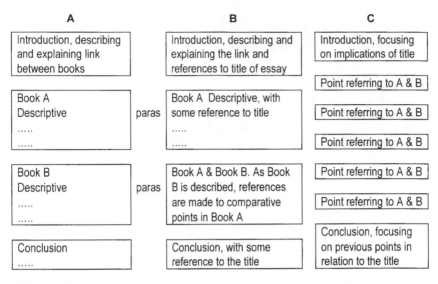

Figure 4

2. The use of rewards

There was a clear recognition that the school's rewards system, involving merits for good work and effort, was favouring the girls' approach to work. Girls, with their better presentation and a more extensive writing style, were being given more merits than boys of similar ability. This resulted in the boys' cynicism about the whole process of rewards and reduced motivation, which was reinforced by the tendency of a number of staff to give merits to poorly behaved boys who worked quietly in the lessons. To address this issue, the rewards policy was revisited to encourage staff to recognise the skills boys brought to their work, i.e. concise answers, more speculative thinking and new ideas, and to be more consistent with regard to the awarding of merits. Clear guidance was set out in the new policy and the giving of merits was carefully monitored. Each individual child was set a target for merits and form tutors liaised with parents on progress. As a result, the balance of merit awards changed and more middle ability and able boys secured high numbers.

3. Use of mixed gender groupings

Having looked closely at the work being undertaken locally on the use of single sex groupings within mixed schools, we believed this was not an appropriate option for our situation for a number of reasons:

- whilst enabling gender specific teaching to be undertaken in single sex groups, the strengths each sex brings to the lesson would be lost, i.e. less speculative thinking in girls' groups and less reflective thinking in all boys groups

- our experience of single sex groups, where these existed through the option structures, was not very successful

- the approach was, in our opinion, unproven

- pragmatically, in a six-form entry school it is very difficult to enable setting and options within single sex groupings.

As a result, we decided to focus our efforts on ensuring the learning experience in the classroom utilised the strengths of both genders' natural learning styles by seeking a varied approach to learning in all lessons. A key factor in our approach was the emphasis on the teacher deciding the pupil groupings in the classroom. (We had previously identified the single sex nature of many apparently mixed teaching groups, a phenomenon recognisable to many teachers). Each learning activity had to be matched to an appropriate pupil grouping. If the activity required problem-solving techniques, then a boy-girl seating strategy was employed. In more practical work, social groupings may be employed and for whole class discussion single sex groupings were utilised. This engendered a learning-centred approach to the classroom experience and greatly affected the pupil behaviour in lessons. The expectation of the pupils was more about learning and less socially orientated. We believed it crucial to have a balance of gender groupings and a variety of activities.

A key part of the approach was to vary the grouping strategy and learning style employed. Staff were surprised at how willing pupils were to work in these groups and the positive impact they had on pupil motivation and behaviour. A very important aspect was the re-evaluation of the learning strategies employed in light of the awareness of the gender specific preferred learning styles. It legitimised a review of teaching styles amongst very experienced teachers, some of whom were set in their ways.

To support this approach, we also examined the gender imbalance in many of our teaching groups. These were particularly prevalent in top Language and Maths sets, but also to our surprise in a number of mixed ability groups in other subjects. Our concern was that these sets often represented the effort of the pupils prior to setting, not their ability, and therefore reinforced underachievement. The very process of examining the issue proved to be a useful staff development and the outcome was a whole school policy on a maximum 65%-35% gender imbalance in all pupil groupings. This left certain subjects with the challenge of raising their subject's appeal in the eyes of one gender!

4. Development of a reading policy

As stated earlier, our empirical research had highlighted the significant gap in reading skills of boys and girls on arrival at the school. Through a selection of interviews and surveys, it became apparent that this problem was exasperated by the boys' limited interest in reading. Only a very small number read for pleasure and this was rarely.

The school embarked on an approach, with the support of our main primary feeder, aimed at raising interest in reading amongst boys or, at the very least, increasing the amount of time they devoted to reading. The strategies, which were brought together into a coherent policy, included:

• reviewing the fiction used in English lessons to ensure boys interests were better catered for

• increasing the range of fiction in the school library to include more science fiction, adventure, horror and sport, which they clearly preferred

• encouraging the English Department to widen their ideas (rather than be dismissive) on what was worthwhile and interesting for boys to read, which required a detailed (and difficult) search for challenging, developmental boys' literature

• working with all staff on how to teach reading and requiring them to focus on the development of reading skills as part of their Key Stage 3 curriculum (we were amazed that one primary head admitted he had never been trained in the teaching of reading)

- alerting all staff to various strategies they could employ to help pupils access the texts employed in their teaching

- involving parent volunteers and older pupils (particular boys) in regular paired reading with boys who were having difficulties.

5. Development of a Compact

A significant number of our middle to low ability boys – the ones we most wanted to target – did not wish to continue in education after 16 and, therefore, were not convinced that GCSEs really mattered. To try to change this culture, we worked with the local TEC to establish a team of mentors from local business to meet regularly with pupils to discuss their work, aspirations and emphasise the importance of formal qualification. A training programme on mentoring techniques was undertaken by all mentors and as a result the majority formed very effective relationships. The different perspective they brought and the creditability they had in the eyes of the pupils was very helpful in lifting motivation and expectations. The difficulties arose in ensuring the team of mentors gave sufficient priority to the role and did not let the pupils down. Not surprisingly, the pupils involved had a low tolerance of mentors who cancelled agreed times without warning!

6. Seeking the pupils' views

Throughout the whole programme, a principle adopted by the group was the involvement of the pupils' views in the selection of the approaches. Extensive use was made of pupil perception surveys, utilising the Keele University Pupil Learning Experience Survey, amongst others, which highlighted the preferred learning styles of boys and girls in a range of curriculum areas. In a number of key areas, pupils were interviewed to gain more qualitative data on the success of various approaches. We found it particularly helpful to employ advisory staff in this role, as the pupils were generally more frank with adults they did not recognise as teachers, but who had extensive experience of communicating with young people.

This level of consultation gave the pupils a clear message that they had an active not passive role in the school's efforts to raise boys' achievement. Too often the pupils are the last group to have 'a say'. As Fullan (1991) suggests:

Students, even little ones, are people too. Unless they have some meaningful (to them) role in the enterprise, most educational change, indeed most education, will fail. I ask the reader not to think of students as running the school, but to entertain the following question: 'What would happen if we treated the student as someone whose opinion mattered in the introduction and implementation of reform in schools?'

Our consultations with pupils offered powerful data for teaching staff, as well as identifying areas for further consideration.

The message from our work

We found the whole project a very positive way to convince staff to look again at the learning experiences in their classroom, and it certainly proved less threatening than an OFSTED inspection. The principles we would recommend for anyone undertaking a similar project are:

- the importance of involving all staff

- the advantage of using research methodology and supporting work with other research studies

- the variety of teaching and learning styles matters more than structural change

- involving pupils in the change creates a sense of ownership and responsibility as well as a team approach

- tackling boy's underachievement requires a new definition of equality of opportunity.

Acknowledgements

We would like to record our thanks to Susan Moss and Jenny Fincken for their contribution of the templates.

Appendix 1
Science Coursework Investigation

The following is a guide through the information you should include in your investigation.

The Problem
Your teacher will discuss with you the topic you are going to investigate.

The investigation has <u>four</u> parts. You will be marked separately on each part.

PLANNING – 8 marks
<u>Think</u> about the <u>problem</u>.

Write a <u>title</u>.

Write a list of the <u>factors/variables</u> which have an effect.

You will need to investigate one factor in <u>detail</u> and obtain <u>reliable results</u>.

Which <u>factor/variable</u> could you investigate?

Now write a <u>prediction</u> for this factor/variable. It needs to be <u>mathematical</u> if possible, e.g. 'If I double the _____ then I expect the _____ to double'.

A prediction is without value unless you explain the <u>theory</u> on which it is based.

<u>Explain</u> 'because I know _____, I can predict that _____'.

It is possible to draw a graph to show what you expect to happen. This will help.

OBTAINING EVIDENCE – 8 marks
You will need a <u>plan</u>.

Think about:

How you will make your method a <u>fair test</u> of the predictions that you have made?

Which <u>factors/variables</u> are you <u>changing</u>?

<u>How many</u> changes will you be making?

What <u>range</u> will these changes cover?

<u>How many times</u> will you make each change?

List the <u>variables</u> that you must <u>control</u>.

How are you going to <u>measure</u> what happens in your investigation?

How will you make your measurements as <u>accurate</u> as possible?

What will you have to do to make sure that you work <u>safely</u>?

How will you record your <u>observations</u> and <u>measurements</u>?

Is there a <u>second method</u> that you could use to <u>check your results</u>?

Now write your <u>METHOD</u>. It should be possible for someone else to carry out your method by reading your instructions.

Do not forget to explain how you will record your <u>observations</u> and <u>measurements</u>.

Do not forget to explain any <u>second method</u> you could use.

CARRY OUT YOUR INVESTIGATION AND RECORD YOUR RESULTS.

ANALYSING EVIDENCE AND DRAWING CONCLUSIONS – 8 marks
Think about your results carefully.

Have you chosen the best method of <u>displaying your results</u>?

Is there a <u>better</u> way of displaying your results?

Is there any <u>pattern</u> to your results?

Do any of your results <u>fail to fit the general pattern</u>?

How do the results compare with your <u>prediction</u>?

How do your results compare with any <u>additional information</u> available to you?

Write a <u>conclusion</u> that is based on your results.

Now use your <u>scientific knowledge</u> to try to <u>explain your results</u>.

EVALUATING THE EVIDENCE – 6 marks
How <u>reliable</u> are your results?

Have you taken enough <u>observations/measurements</u>?

List anything in your investigation that may have led to <u>errors</u>.

Were you <u>justified</u> in drawing your <u>conclusion</u> or did the <u>problems</u> with the method make the <u>conclusion unreliable</u>?

Are there any ways in which you could have <u>improved</u> your investigation?

What <u>additional experiments</u> could you carry out that might provide <u>further evidence</u> to make you more <u>sure of your conclusion</u>?

References

Arnold R (1997): *Raising Levels of Achievement in Boys*. Slough, Education Management Information Exchange (NFER).

Balding J (1994): *Young People in 1993*. Exeter, Schools Health Education Unit (Exeter University).

Bray R, Gardner C, Parsons N, Downes P and Hannan G (1997): *Can Boys do Better?* Leicester, SHA.

Downes P (1994): The gender effect. *Managing Schools Today*, 3 (5), 7-8.

Fullan M (1991): *The New Meaning of Educational Change*. London, Cassell.

Licht B G and Dweck C (1987): Sex differences in achievement orientations. In Arnot G and Weiner G (Eds): *Gender and the Politics of Schooling*. London, Hutchinson.

Warrington M and P (1996): Gender and achievement: the debate at GCSE. *Education Review*, 10(1), 22-27.

Wheatley J (1996): Outclassed. *The Times* Magazine, 30/3/96, 17-20.

8

Peer Counselling at The Boswells School, Chelmsford

John Ryder

The whole school context

At The Boswells School in Chelmsford, we have long been concerned about the imbalance of achievement between boys and girls. For a dozen years and more, this has shown itself, not only in the more objective way of differential examination results, but also in the premature disaffection of the boys from the educational process generally. An analysis of the half-termly progress reports for Year 9 in October 1995 indicated boys receiving a total of 346 positive marks, whereas girls received 553. The girls were given 19 negative marks as opposed to 86 for the boys. These results, on a simple count up, were not only highly significant statistically, but they also confirmed our long-held view that boys were turning off school in their droves, and that this would continue to contribute to the problem of differentiated achievement.

The Boswells is a large, urban comprehensive school, with eight forms of reasonably balanced entry and a Sixth Form of about 270 students. The GCSE results in the summer of 1995 showed a 5+ A*-C rate of 66% overall, with 82% for the girls and 49% for the boys. Faced with a strong drive to improve standards both nationally and within the school, the time was clearly right for a significant initiative in this area. Head of Year, Dave Morrish, and Head of English, Richard May, both allocated an hour a week of curriculum development time in the 1996-97 academic year, were joined by Deputy Head, John Ryder, in an attempt to make serious inroads with this most complex and intractable issue.

We decided that the time for further research and additional audits was past – what was needed were practical actions and clear strategies that could be adopted in order to turn the situation around. But which to try? The current literature was extensive and rather daunting. We decided on a year's trial of the widest range of initiatives that we could devise. The whole staff would then evaluate these at a non-pupil day at the end of the year, and either continue or scrap them as appropriate.

Peer counselling, the subject of this chapter, had already run once in the summer of 1996 and it was decided to continue this along with all the other initiatives. To understand fully, therefore, the context of the peer counselling, it is first necessary to mention briefly the other strategies that have been introduced.

Monitoring and evaluation. We latched onto a scheme already in existence, where an hour a week is allocated to Heads of Skill Areas for Monitoring and Evaluation. Guidelines were issued focusing this activity on aspects such as expectations of boys, setting of standards, male-orientated learning experiences, short-term targets, and extensive use of praise – designed, it was stressed, to change staff practice.

Representatives in skill areas. A small group of enthusiastic staff across the areas was recruited to raise the gender question at meetings or in discussion whenever relevant topics were under scrutiny. These might include such issues as setting, methods of assessment, use of ICT, schemes of work, and choice of syllabus.

Boy/girl seating. It has always seemed anomalous that, with so much about the education process being highly prescriptive, we so often simply allow the students to sit where they like. We knew that boys and girls learn in different ways. Might not they learn from each other in a mutually beneficial way? Given that many students set their standards of work and behaviour by reference to their peers, the example of a hard-working, well-behaved girl might cause some boys to re-examine their notorious and ill-judged optimism, and raise their sights. Quite a few groups, mainly at KS3, were piloted with this seating arrangement.

Work with primary schools. Research seemed to show that patterns of underachievement of reading and writing are set very early. A boy who is significantly behind by age seven will probably never catch up. The attitude and involvement of parents in the earliest years is paramount. So, working through our feeder primary schools, we organised an evening event for the reception year parents (i.e. parents of four-year-olds). Over 200, a majority of them fathers, attended an evening at The Boswells. This included a brief look at the *Panorama* programme *The Future is Female*, a primary and secondary perspective, and an inspiring address from Wendy Cooling on the delights and importance of books and reading as a shared experience.

Year 11 targeting of underachievers. This has been in place now for a number of years, mainly carried out by senior staff. It was decided to extend this into Years 12 and 13 for the first time. It runs parallel to, and in support of, our very well developed pastoral structure.

Mentoring in Year 10. As an experiment, a small group of under-achievers, identified through the skill areas, have been allowed to choose a mentor from all staff within the school. Careful guidelines were issued, and parents involved. The value of this approach clearly lay with the strength of the relationship between student and adult.

Methods of assessment. At staff briefings, we were at pains to try to get colleagues to take as broad a view of assessment as possible. The boy who is keen with practical work, and is the first to answer a question orally in class, deserves recognition for his effort as much as the girl who submits three pages of well-presented script. If it was important to praise boys in class (five 'pats' to every one 'slap'), it was surely equally important that we continued the emphasis on praise in our more formal progress reports. We needed to change the culture from criticism to praise.

Peer pressure and school ethos. This is a really tough nut to crack – boys hiding their lights under bushels to avoid negative peer pressure. It is present in school, not only in the obvious academic field, but also in music, drama and even sport. We were determined, as an institution, to be even more positive in our celebration of success. A new 'Achievements' notice board in the staffroom feeds through to Year assemblies, where individuals, groups, classes, teams or sometimes the whole year group receive praise and positive feedback on the achievements of the week. Each week, in addition, a particularly worthwhile achievement, either from inside or outside the school, is highlighted on the school achievement board. All channels at our disposal were to be used to see that achievement, in its broadest sense, was always celebrated and applauded, and never sneered at or decried.

Work within skill areas. A great deal of attention has been focused on areas where the achievement of boys most seriously lagged behind that of girls (notably in English and Modern Languages). As a consequence, a whole variety of strategies are being attempted, and good practice built on. These include, in English for example, ten minutes silent reading at the start of each lesson; a constant review of the gender balance of reading material available in the department and in the library; a renewed emphasis on handwriting; the breaking up of lessons into shorter timed activities with immediate targets; the issuing of clear, careful and concrete systems to aid essay writing, and many more.

It is into this context of a plethora of other initiatives across the school that the introduction of a modest scheme of peer counselling should be considered.

Timing of the scheme

Given the range of other activities, it was decided that the latter part of Year 9 was an appropriate time for the project. The question of timing was an important one. Was the summer term of Year 9 too late for some boys, who had already shown marked deterioration since the end of Year 8? After all, a great deal of current thought says that it is towards the end of Year 8 that many boys start to become disaffected. On the other hand, given the fairly adult approach required to the setting up of a rapport with a sixth-form student, was any earlier practicable? Wouldn't lack of maturity (possibly on both sides) mean that the programme might fail to achieve its objectives? Then again, what about the situation of the Lower Sixth students we were proposing to use? Could a time be found when they were established in their courses and not under undue pressure themselves from other directions?

Another linked issue of timing was how long should the activity continue? Too short, and it would have only limited impact; too long, and it would make too extensive a demand on the counsellors. In the end, it was decided to commence the project at half-term in the spring term, to run until the end of the summer term.

What did we wish to achieve?

The scope of the project was to be quite modest – about a dozen under-achieving boys from Year 9 were to be paired with the same number of male students from Year 12. The aims of the work were ambitious, indeed – primarily, to exert a major effect on the motivation and general attitude to school work of the Year 9 students and subsequently, of course, their levels of achievement at GCSE, A-levels and beyond. There were also hoped-for knock-on effects for the rest of the year group. After all, most of those selected were by their very nature quite influential amongst their peers. Who could say what effect positive changes amongst twelve such boys might have on others? The theory of critical mass, borrowed from science, can often be perceived in action amongst groups of youngsters. Once it is moving in the right direction, much can follow. There were also expected gains for the Year 12 counsellors, as well. To be selected and trusted with such an important responsibility and to carry it out with some reliability and success surely says something about the young adult concerned. UCAS references were already being redrafted to reflect this! The bonus for the teaching staff was that here was an initiative being tried that would hopefully enable one or more of their students to be more motivated and committed, and all without any input of time or effort on their part!

It is important to state at this time that the focus of the counselling was seen to be firmly in the realm of helping the selected pupil to improve his motivation towards schoolwork, and thus enhance his academic achievement. It was never designed to be counselling in its widest sense – an opportunity for youngsters with serious problems of social maladjustment to unburden themselves to untrained students only three years older than themselves. As a school, we always stress that our excellent pastoral system exists, not to sort out students' home lives, but to enable them to achieve their potential in school. The guidelines for peer counselling were to be very much the same. To expect anything more of our sixth-formers would be both unfair and unwise.

Planning, and selection of students

The planning for the project took place over the previous few months and involved in the first instance the Head of Year 9, his assistant Head of Year, the Head of the Sixth Form, and Deputy Head. Initial discussions focused on issues such as the aims of the exercise, the selection of students, the involvement of parents, the briefing of both sets of students, the production of guidelines, the production of written material and the structure of interviews and meetings. There were also more practical considerations such as where were pairs to meet, how often, and when during the day. Subsequently, and particularly over the issue of selection of participants, teams of tutors in both year-groups were also involved.

The selection of the Year 9 students was carried out in consultation with the eight tutors of that year-group. We were looking to identify about twelve underachieving male students, who we thought could potentially benefit from peer counselling. These were likely to be reasonably able students who were failing to display a lot of untapped potential. Although, as a consequence, they probably experienced some behavioural difficulties in class, we were not setting out simply to identify the twelve 'worst' boys in the year group. Whilst this may have been tempting, probably it would have been unrealistic to expect major behaviour modification in that particular cohort. Finally, since a degree of parental support was to be elicited, it was important to choose students where we thought this involvement would be forthcoming. Twelve Year 9 students were duly selected.

The production of a group of suitable Year 12 students went on concurrently, following the same pattern. Suggestions were forthcoming from the Sixth Form tutors and agreed with the Head of Year. The criteria this time were obviously different. The ideal counsellor would be male, *with a hint of underachievement in his own record*, but who had nevertheless come good, and was now firmly established in the Sixth Form with reasonable academic prospects. It was someone who had faced all the pressures and temptations to under-perform in Year 9 and had come through them. This would give him more empathy and 'street-cred' with his client than a teacher or parent could possibly have – and maybe, therefore, more influence. Clearly, the students concerned would have to want to participate in the scheme. Pleasingly, having been selected and invited to take part, and having had the opportunity to give something back to the school pointed out to them, all were happy to participate. We had our dozen counsellors.

Parents' involvement

The next stage was to contact the parents of the selected Year 9 students. This was done, not only to keep them informed about what was happening, but also to elicit their support in the programme. It was clearly very important, in an exercise that depended so much on good-will and co-operation to succeed, that there was nothing but positive feelings from the parents towards the scheme. The Head of Year carried this out by telephone, as it gave full opportunity for parents to ask any questions that might occur to them. Careful explanation was given regarding how students were selected, what was planned to happen, and what were the hoped-for outcomes. In most cases, of course, it came as no surprise to most parents that their son had been selected for such a project. Their son's underachievement was not only already well known to them but, along with the school, they had been trying to address the problem for some while. All parents were interested in the scheme and generally pleased with a new initiative designed to bring benefit to their son. They were encouraged to monitor the situation 'from a dis-tance' and keep in touch with the school as things developed. Interest-ingly, several parents showed the same reactions as their sons – that simply having been identified and chosen was a source of pleasure. Parents were also invited into school to discuss the initiative further with the Head of Year if they so wished. This initial contact was fol-lowed up by a formal letter confirming these arrangements.

Briefing of students, and guidelines to be followed

Meanwhile, separate briefing meetings were arranged with the two groups of students concerned. At the Year 9 meeting, the nature of the programme was outlined. The Head of Year explained carefully how and why the students had been selected. The nature and problems of underachievement were stated, as was the fact that their inclusion in such a programme showed that the school really valued them and wanted them to succeed. It was stressed that this was in no way a punishment for previous bad work or behaviour, but an opportunity for them to break into their downward spiral of underachievement. The students were then asked if any wished to opt out of the programme, as it was not compulsory that they participate. None wished to do so; all certainly appeared by their demeanour and attitude to be genuinely interested in the scheme and keen to take part.

Certain guidelines pertaining to meetings and discussions between paired students were covered. These included relatively mundane matters, such as appropriate language: no overt denigration of teachers would be allowed. It also included reference to the more difficult issue of confidentiality. It was pointed out to the students that the counsellors would be instructed that they must never promise 'not to tell anyone'. The Year 12 counsellors were, in that sense, bound by the same rules as members of staff: confidential information received where a young person was clearly at risk would have to be passed on to the Head of Year or his assistant. Finally, self-assessment sheets were distributed to the students. These covered such issues as work habits, completion of homework, behaviour in class, study skills, etc. Students were asked to complete these in their own time in preparation for the next meeting, when they would be allocated their counsellor.

At about the same time, a meeting was convened of the Year 12 counsellors. The aims of this meeting were as follows: to involve the Sixth Form students in active negotiation of their role as peer counsellor; to stress the importance of the task and trust that was being placed in them; to introduce a common set of guidelines for the process; to indicate areas for discussion and appropriate behaviour with the Year 9 students; and to give some elementary hints and techniques to help them with the role of counsellor. The following set of guidelines was issued and discussed:

- appropriate language must be used at all times

- no direct denigration of individual teachers was to be permitted

- there was no need for any personal disclosure from the Sixth Form student unless they were happy to do so

- the conversation should be guided towards a set of outcomes which the counsellor had thought through before the interview

- always meet in a place where you could easily be seen and inter-rupted, e.g. a Head of Year's office

- the conversation should be as positive as possible

- counsellors were duty bound to pass on any confidential information where the young person is at risk to Head of Year 9 or Head of Sixth Form – although no one else should be informed. They must never promise 'not to tell anyone'.

The format of the first interview was to consist of a review of the Year 9 student's progress to date (or lack of it), coupled with a look at their self-assessment sheets. This would culminate in the setting of agreed targets for the student. These targets, which were to be recorded, could be referred to at future meetings. It was stressed that the counsellors could – by using their similarity of experience, talking in 'their sort of language', and giving them advice – save the younger students a great deal of trouble. Simple things like organisation, a 'to do' list and time management techniques should be actively discussed and encouraged.

Of greatest importance, though, was the attitude of the counsellor. Is it really sensible not to work, to get marks below what one could achieve? Who does it impress? How will it help you in later life? Why do you want to underachieve? The counsellor has been through this sort of situation, to some degree, and would be able to advise them of the dangers. These students are not likely to be getting many positive com-ments from teachers, and therefore a useful strategy would be to make supportive comments regarding the targets they have set. The more positive the relationship established, the more chance there is of chang-ing the negative attitude of the student.

The Sixth Form students were to be responsible for arranging the more 'formal' meetings – three or four over the three-month period of the scheme were suggested. These could be fitted in at lunch-times, or a tutorial period could be used if it coincided with the Sixth Former having an administration period. This would ensure that the minimum interruption to timetable would occur. In addition, it was stressed that informal meetings on corridors or in the playground, even at the most basic level of a brief 'how's it going?', played an important part as well.

An evaluation of the exercise

At the end of the summer term, we sat down to evaluate what had been achieved. Ongoing but informal discussions as the scheme had developed suggested that things were progressing without any major hitches. However, as we had suspected from the start, this was not going to be easy to evaluate on any sort of objective basis. Certainly, some target students were showing definite signs of progress, as evidenced by improving progress reports and more positive comments by teachers. Yet who was to say that this was not simply part of a general process of maturation – or maybe it was as a consequence of other initiatives taking place concurrently, or of other more individual and external factors? Equally, other students showed little signs of progress – but might they have regressed further if they had not been involved in the project? We had no scientifically constructed control group with which to make comparisons. What of our initial aim of affecting the critical mass of a whole year group, and thereby improving the performance and work ethic of the whole cohort? We certainly felt quite positive about the year group as a whole by the end of the summer term, but to what extent was this the result of the Peer Counselling programme?

These questions, of course, are impossible to answer, as we knew they would be when we started. The important thing, we felt, was not to become trapped into doing nothing, simply because the process was too complex to measure in any sort of objective way. It was sufficient that staff and both sets of students involved in the process were generally positive in their responses, and had felt it to be worthwhile. It was best, therefore, to let them speak for themselves, especially as teachers were only involved in setting the scheme up, and not in the process itself. It was decided to carry out some in-depth sample interviewing of both sets of students, and also of the parents. This was carried out in the early part of the autumn term.

Two ex-Year 9 students and two ex-Year 12 students were interviewed for approximately 25 minutes each, using a combination of prepared questions and free discussion. The younger students, independently, made the following points:

• they didn't mind being part of the scheme

- they had not been laughed at by their friends for being chosen

- the interviews got easier as they relaxed more

- most of the discussion, and the targets, centred on the issue of homework

- it was much better being told these things by students, rather than by 'sad' teachers

- they definitely improved with their homework as a result

- this improvement had kept going this term as well, and had been noticed by their teachers

- they had now set themselves higher targets for success in GCSE and beyond.

Both youngsters gave the scheme 4 out of 5, and said that they would definitely recommend it to anyone in the new Year 9. They came across as thoughtful, aware of the issues and pleased to have been valued by the school in such an individual way.

The two Sixth Formers, also interviewed individually, both said:

- they had felt quite nervous, particularly at the first meeting

- they had enjoyed being involved, since it was something quite outside their normal experience

- they thought they would have made some difference to the younger students that they were counselling

- they were really pleased to find that this was indeed the case

- they did not find the time or commitment too onerous

- they would recommend it to any other students asked to contribute in the future

- they had both mentioned their involvement in their letter of application to UCAS

- they definitely felt that the scheme should continue.

Parents who were followed up both formally and informally were also convinced of the worthwhile nature of the counselling, and had noticed improvements in their sons' attitude, particularly with regard to home-work. Teachers were able to confirm this improvement. Generally speaking, therefore, participants and observers could see the value of such an arrangement and were all in favour of it continuing for the next year and beyond.

The Way Forward

The future of peer counselling at The Boswells School needs to be seen in the whole-school context of the many initiatives undertaken to raise levels of achievement. At the time of writing, following a very success-ful non-pupil training day held at the school, it has been decided to reflect the strong support of the staff by maintaining and building on the strategies begun in 1996. Peer counselling will continue to run with the new Year 9 cohort.

Considerable thought was given to ensuring that these 'one-off' pilot schemes become firmly embedded into the normal custom and practice of the school. Some will just happen, by the passing on of good practice – a sort of osmosis. One example of this is the technique of boy/girl seating, which has been taken up this academic year quite extensively. Staff liked what they saw and what they heard, and are trying it for themselves. The responsibilities for certain other strategies, however, need to be written into job descriptions. The Year 10 mentoring scheme, for example, will become the remit of the Head of Year 10. In the same way, peer counselling will continue with the Head of Year 9 taking the lead. We intend to run it at the same time of year, and with approxi-mately the same number of students, as previously.

This coming academic year, the issue of underachievement will be kept closely under scrutiny, and the pressure maintained. The fact that 1998-99 has been designated the National Year of Reading should give great impetus to our work in this area throughout the school in general, and in the library in particular. Much work is also going on in the English and Modern Languages skill areas, the two within the school (as nationally) where the discrepancy between the genders is most marked. We are also determined to do our best in the field of staff recruitment.

Just as it is important that women are fairly represented at senior management level, so is it equally vital that male teachers are well in evidence in the English and Modern Languages departments. We shall also continue rigorously to apply our setting policy, which allows for a maximum and minimum proportion of each gender in all teaching groups. In addition, we must ensure that the issue of underachievement is kept at the forefront of parents' consciousness. At all public occasions when parents come into the school – new Year 7 evening, Year 9 options, etc. – reference will be made to this topic.

Finally, the school has determined that the raising of achievement is so fundamental to the purposes of the school that it will feature prominently in every teacher's biennial appraisal. One of the two designated focuses of all appraisals will be 'raising achievement levels in my classes.' As we move towards the millennium, underachievement remains one of the key issues facing the nation as a whole, and schools and teachers individually. Raising awareness, identification of the problem, and debating causes are only the first and easiest steps on a long road. Only time will tell whether we can reverse the current trends.

9

Teaching boys and girls in separate classes at Shenfield High School, Brentwood

Beverley Swan

To the casual observer, watching the pupils enter the playground and mill around, chatting and playing, awaiting the 8.40 a.m. morning bell, Shenfield High School in Brentwood would appear to be much the same as any other mixed comprehensive school in a middle-class, suburban neighbourhood. If this casual observer were to follow students firstly to their lockers, and then on to form rooms for registration and collective worship, the same perception would prevail. However, when the nine o'clock bell sounds for the start of lessons, the uniqueness of the school becomes apparent as the boys filter off to their lessons in one direction, and the girls to theirs in another. For in September 1994, Shenfield High School embarked upon a brave, new initiative to teach boys and girls in separate classes in every subject.

We had tried something similar before, but focused only on science. The now retired Head, Dr Peter Osborne, a physicist himself, had been debating an article in *The Guardian* that declared: 'There is very little doubt that the answer to Britain's inability to produce enough scientists and technologists lies in the hands of the girls. They form a pool of talent that either cannot or will not follow scientific courses towards careers!' It was from this debate that Shenfield's first initiative, Girls Into Science and Technology or GIST, was born. The objective was to make the physical sciences more attractive to girls. Little did we think at the time that such a modest experiment would eventually lead to such significant changes; nor that there would be a reversal of public concern, from primarily helping girls, to helping boys!

The 1985 strategy to increase opportunities for girls to succeed in science lessons initially involved positive discrimination in favour of girls at the expense of the boys. Girls replaced boys on the front benches. They were encouraged to answer questions, select their equipment before the boys and to conduct their own experiments, rather than being relegated to recording neatly the results! To counter this negative discrimination against boys, the initiative led in the following year to the experiment of a single-sex class each for boys and girls for GCSE physics. For girls, this was very successful. For boys, it produced a lively group, difficult to control, but not an insurmountable problem, and possibly the result of particular personalities rather than a feature of the single-sex structure. GIST was discontinued when it was overtaken by the advent of the National Curriculum, which made science compulsory for all pupils. It had, however, succeeded in increasing the number of girls planning to study physics in Year 10 and Year 11. The lesson learned was reflected in a later bid by the Information Technology Department to increase girls' interest in this subject by operating a girls-only computer club night.

The pendulum swings

By the early 1990s, the pendulum of concern began to swing from girls to boys. The findings of Professor Michael Barber of Keele University indicated that, despite 70 per cent of teacher time being given to boys, and despite girls professing to feelings of academic inferiority compared to the boys, girls were achieving *better* results than boys in most GCSE subjects. It was at this point that Dr Osborne began to look again at the early initiatives at Shenfield. Clearly, the emphasis now needed to be on how to address the under-achievement of boys, whilst enabling the girls to recognise and utilise their potential; yet, this time, whatever system the school adopted must *not* involve positive discrimination in favour of one sex against the other. Hence, there evolved the idea of educating boys and girls separately in every subject (not just Science), whilst retaining the social benefits of a mixed school.

The thinking behind the move was concerned primarily with government pressure to produce better results, linked with the publication of the league tables. Also, the six local comprehensive schools in Brentwood were, at that time, locked into a highly competitive situation where marketing and promotion were intense. A perceived bonus to the implementation of the new initiative was that, by making Shenfield High School identifiable from the rest, we could afford to be less active within the expensive and often negative marketing framework. There would be a unique, positive reason for selecting our school. Dr Osborne viewed the move to single-sex classes as not a major issue when set beside an earlier philosophical shift from mixed ability grouping to banding pupils according to ability. This initiative was, in his opinion, just part of the strategy to deliver the requirements of the National Curriculum by targeted teaching. It would, he hoped, enable the school to produce better results whilst taking itself sideways out of the marketing rat race.

The micro-politics of change

Having researched his idea, and decided that this was the way forward for the school, the Head realised that its acceptance and adoption by the Board of Governors, staff, parents and pupils would require careful management. Confidentiality would be a key factor in the early days. In January 1993, he put the plan to his two Deputy Heads, who visited nearby Moulsham High. This is a mixed school which had taught boys and girls in separate classes since it was created out of the amalgamation of two single-sex schools when the area went comprehensive in the early 1970s. The Deputy Heads discussed the system with Moulsham teachers and investigated the interaction of the pupils, the cost and timetable implications. The process convinced one Deputy, but not the other! The next stage was to raise the idea with the Chair of Governors, and thereafter, in early July, with the Chairs of the Governors' sub-committees. The senior management team was to follow. By mid-July, some fourteen or fifteen people knew of the proposal and had subjected it to very probing examination and, by some, to a degree of reservation!

The Department for Education had been approached to see if the model needed to be written into the forthcoming proposal for Grant Maintained status. They stated that it was an internal matter and did not need any approval. At the end of July, the move was still secret, since Governors had not approved it. Dr Osborne was clear that its announcement needed to be carefully controlled and timed for October 1993 to coincide with the advertisement for the school's prospective parents evening. Total confidentiality was necessary to prevent rumours and misconceived ideas undermining the successful launch of the initiative. It was not necessary to consult existing parents, since none of the children already attending Shenfield would be directly involved. The plan was to take effect from the 1994 intake onwards, with the remainder of the school retaining its mixed nature as it progressed through to Year 11.

The process of informing the body of the staff started at the beginning of the autumn term. The initiative was announced to senior teachers. Departmental heads were requested to make their opinions known to Heads of Faculty, who were then asked to prepare written statements of their colleagues' responses for the full governing body. Following Governors' approval, the decision to 'go single-sex' was announced at a full staff meeting. It was not presented as a matter for discussion but as a formally taken decision, backed by research and evidence.

Although this outline of events presents the process as one that gained general consent, it was by no means straightforward or universally approved. Astonishment and scepticism from the body of staff greeted the announcement. There was no outright hostility, but much quiet discussion was generated about the wisdom of the move, how it would be accepted by parents and pupils and, indeed, how the initiative would be delivered and managed.

Under the media spotlight

It was the media reaction to the announcement that really took the school by storm. A brief outline of the new arrangement was sent to the local press, but it was the nationals who exhibited so much interest. *The Sun* was the first. A telephone call at 10.00 a.m. on the following day was followed two hours later by the arrival of a photographer. From then on, the school telephone lines were engaged almost continuously and it was clear that the modest press release had been 'leaked' to the national media. Articles appeared in all the national newspapers except the *Financial Times*.

Interest must have been linked to the recently published league tables that indicated not only the success of single-sex schools, but also the underachievement of boys. Perhaps there was even a perception by the right wing tabloids that this must be an aspect of 'Back to Basics', which was the political buzz of the moment. Radio and television reporters were quick to take up the theme. On one occasion, there were no fewer than three TV crews filming in different classes at the same time, causing one Year 11 student to comment that he 'fully expected to see Kate Adie round a corner, complete with flak jacket'. Indeed, such was the intensity of the invasion that the school seriously considered pulling up the drawbridge.

The last intake of the old system coped with confidence and fortitude, for it was the (still co-educational) Year 7 who took the brunt of the questioning. The potential for damaging reports was immense. There had been carefully laid plans to inform existing parents and pupils of the impending changes prior to the publication of the news in the local press. The 'leak' and swift uptake of the story by the national media meant that these plans had been pre-empted. The first that many students knew of the initiative was when the lights were switched on and the microphone was thrust under their noses!

There was no time for priming. Our pupils did not let us down. Our faith in them was justified by their loyalty. They sometimes acknowledged that the opposite sex could be a distraction in the classroom; however, they came down firmly on the side of mixed classes. This was hardly surprising, as it was the only system they had experienced. Nonetheless, the programmes produced took a very positive view of the plans and we received some good publicity. One chastening thought came to us from a senior pupil. If single-sex classes are so good, perhaps existing pupils were having to make do with second best. We had to acknowledge this viewpoint and ponder the delivery of lessons to all our pupils.

After this initial limelight, we were left in peace to make our arrangements whilst interest and debate about the academic performance of boys and girls continued around us. Underachievement of boys and the single-sex question certainly became an educational 'hot potato'.

Checks and balances

For the 1994 intake, boys and girls would be placed in single-sex form groups and in broad academic bands for their single-sex lessons in all subjects. My own thought, as Head of Lower School, was that a consequence of the new system was the loss of the social advantages of mixed classes. Would there be a need to compensate for this? Of course, pupils would have the usual opportunities to mix in the playground, on the buses to and from school, and in recreation clubs. Yet I wanted to place greater emphasis on activities that would enable pupils to interact together in a purposeful way, to see each other as working partners as well as social contacts. It was important, in my view, to build a pastoral programme of ventures where pupils operated in mixed groups. A School Council was set up and embarked upon the organisation of debates, quizzes, competitions and visits. A Christmas Tea Party for a group of local senior citizens involved a large number of pupils in cooking, entertaining, preparing gifts and hosting the event. In addition, our extra-curricular clubs continued to be well supported by boys and girls and provided a variety of opportunities for mixed activities. Most notable amongst these was Sports Night, where pupils could participate in a wide variety of games for recreation rather than competition.

It was projected that this arrangement would exist throughout Key Stage 3, but with modifications at Key Stage 4. English, Mathematics and Science would remain as single sex lessons, but the remainder of subjects would be taught in co-educational groups. Not only would this offer the benefit of a gradual re-integration before Sixth Form or College study, which would be totally mixed, but it would also be cost effective for the minority subjects where it was clear that two single sex groups could not be supported.

In our presentation to prospective parents, a balance had to be made. Recent publication of examination results had shown that the traditional superiority at 16-plus of girls in certain subjects was beginning to increase. Girls were not only doing better than the boys in subjects traditionally considered to be their stronger areas, such as Languages, but were also beginning to catch up, and in some cases out-perform, them in Mathematics, Science and Technology – subjects in which boys usually flourished. It would be easy to demonstrate the advantages to girls of single-sex classes, but what was in it for the boys?

Parents were shown research (much of it referred to elsewhere in this book) indicating that, in comparison with girls, boys

- are less happy at school

- are less motivated

- do less work

- behave less well

- take up to 70 per cent of the teacher time.

It was pointed out that single-sex classes for boys would

- take away the audience (girls)

- enable lessons to be more interesting

- create a boy-centred atmosphere

- allow us to find out why boys do not like school.

Although girls were getting the results, they were still not taking advantage of their head start. Our presentation highlighted research revealing that girls

- think they get less praise

- think they are less able

- become less motivated

- are made to feel undervalued by boys.

Single-sex classes for girls, therefore, would

- promote self-esteem and confidence

- promote involvement

- promote motivation

- provide opportunities for girls to take responsibility and make decisions

- offer opportunities for leadership.

Throughout, we stressed our commitment to both sexes and the co-educational nature of the school's social organisation. Our new initiative would permit the development of girls and development of boys to be fostered and allow them each to achieve their true and best academic level of ability, whilst enabling them also to interact and integrate socially. We thought that it would provide the best of both worlds. It was on the basis of this final plan that Year 6 parents were invited to make their choice. Undoubtedly, one of the key factors in measuring success would be the uptake of places for the first year of the new initiative. We held our breath and waited!

Policy into practice

The LEA forecast for the intake for 1994 was 140 children. 164 pupils were admitted to Shenfield High School in September. This was deemed to be not an enormous increase, but a significant one. Parents subjected us to some searching questions, particularly those who already had children in the school. Being satisfied with the status quo, they wondered what effect the changes would have. From the over-whelming numbers that came to 'hear all about it', and the modest increase in the intake, we can assume that there were others who adopted a 'wait and see' attitude.

It had been recognised, early in the planning, that there could be an imbalance of boys compared to girls applying to join the school. This could inject significant new costs as a direct consequence of single-sex teaching. This cost was made apparent in the very first year, when the first intake yielded 72 girls and 92 boys. In the past, these 164 boys and girls would have been split into six co-educational forms, each of 27 or 28 children. This time they were split into three girls' forms (of 24) and four boys' forms (of 23) – costing the school the salary of the additional 1.15 FTE staff needed to teach the extra class. We were prepared to accept this additional cost as the price worth paying for the advantages of the scheme. Smaller classes, anyway, were a benefit in themselves.

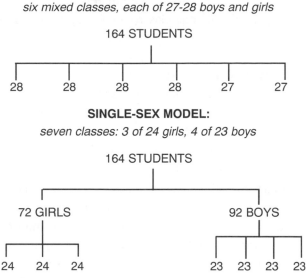

CO-EDUCATIONAL MODEL:

six mixed classes, each of 27-28 boys and girls

164 STUDENTS

| 28 | 28 | 28 | 28 | 27 | 27 |

SINGLE-SEX MODEL:

seven classes: 3 of 24 girls, 4 of 23 boys

164 STUDENTS

72 GIRLS   92 BOYS

| 24 | 24 | 24 | | 23 | 23 | 23 | 23 |

Once again, in September 1994, the media spotlight focused itself upon our school. As the new pupils assembled in the playground, *Panorama* cameras caught the action. With one sweep of her arm, like Moses parting the waves, the Deputy Head of Lower School divided the intake: girls to the left and boys to the right. We were off on our new programme! I have to confess that despite the significance of the moment when these pupils arrived for their first lesson with me, I began in the way I had done for all previous Septembers in my teaching career. I had read the research and discussed the pros and cons of the new system at length with friends and colleagues. Yet I had no experience or training in single-sex teaching, in either my own education or career. No new classroom strategies were in place, and it was very much left to the individual to find his/her own way with the new initiative.

Perhaps, on reflection, this is the only way it could have been. Often, we teachers have skills we fail to recognise: one is that we make adjustments and tailor our style and material to the needs, nature and ability of whatever group we face, whether mixed or single sex. To do otherwise in this situation may have been to start from a false premise. For the Year 7 pupils the day was going to be a big one, in any case. They took the added scrutiny by the media as just another part of it. The rest of the school was far more agog at the cameras than the sight of an all-boys class waiting outside one classroom as an all-girls class departed from it!

The change becomes the norm

In April 1995, just two terms later, Dr Osborne retired as planned, and the task of further development and refinement fell to the new Head, John Fairhurst. He was able to offer much advice and experience gained from his previous post as Deputy Head of Moulsham High School although, as he said, his former school had been born, some twenty years earlier, with its 'sexual arrangements' given by God (well, the LEA, at any rate!). Just like the rest of us, Moulsham took these arrangements for granted, as an unchallengeable assumption of its life. Shenfield, however, was undergoing a 'sex change' and needed to think about what it was doing very much more closely! Accordingly, the new Head listened carefully to the views, not only of the pupils but also the parents and the staff. It soon emerged that there was general agreement we could further enhance the two-fold benefits of single-sex lessons in a mixed environment by making form groups – part of the *social* side of school life – co-educational. This change was effected in September 1996 for all the years in Key Stage 3.

By this stage, even senior pupils initially resistant to the change accepted the new style at Shenfield High School as the norm. Sixth Formers who assisted with Lower School activities could see little change in pupils' interaction from their own mixed experience. Those involved expressed positive views. Both boys and girls said they felt they could be more open in class. They were not so concerned about what the others were thinking or saying about them. In Personal and Social Education classes, they could focus on topics that more directly concerned them. They had more opportunities in class for making friends and forming teams. Girls reported that they missed the boys because they made the lessons more fun, but they could concentrate and participate more! Boys said they could get on without the girls whispering and putting pressure on them. There is, of course, continued debate whether, for example, one offers boys *Julius Caesar* and girls *Romeo and Juliet* for study. Should we pander to gender-based taste or extend it? In any case, we are always mindful of the dangers of generalisations.

Interestingly, the boys seem *more* prepared to participate in discussions of literature, poetry, religious and moral issues in all-male groups. Such acknowledgement, by boys, of their emotional and spiritual lives is, in our view, a positive outcome of major import and significant evidence that we are *not* simply pandering to 'macho' stereotypes. As for the question of integration, all pupils replied that they had made friends with a new person of the opposite sex. They had been introduced in the playground or at clubs and extra curricular activities within the Lower School.

To staff, patterns were beginning to emerge. It has become starkly obvious to us that boys and girls learn very, very differently. Teachers could not be as positive about their experiences as the pupils. Whilst many found girls' classes a delight, with students keen and willing to tackle tasks diligently and present work thoroughly and neatly, boys' classes were much more difficult to manage. Lessons were noisier and pupils more challenging in every respect. Staff who had been ambivalent towards the initiative were, in some cases, becoming disillusioned. I organised a number of lunchtime meetings and established that the main problems were occurring in the boys' lower band. The same half dozen names were mentioned by teachers of this group.

Of course, these six boys would have presented a challenge in mixed classes. Under our system, however, they were concentrated into just one group. Also, with fewer classes for each sex, the setting/banding system was necessarily not as fine and the range of ability within any one class was bound to be greater, taxing the differentiation skills of some teachers. We needed to address the problems quickly enough to halt staff fears, and prevent the erosion of a good work ethic within the class.

We resolved to tighten our discipline, something that naturally followed from the change of Head and a number of other key personnel. In general, the boys responded, for example, to the same routine for entry into classrooms, and to a new school-wide code of clear and concise instructions. They work best when given short-term targets and a variety of tasks with different approaches within the same lesson. They like a challenge and enjoy competition. We also felt that it was important to give these boys greater contact with male teachers, since many of them lack male role models in their lives. Where the gender of the teacher had never been a timetabling issue when our school was co-educational, due thought was given to this and seen to pay dividends.

Our attentions to the lower ability boys groups gradually began to pay off, but we continue to re-visit and re-evaluate. We were (and still are) all aware of the steep learning curve on which we have embarked. Occasionally, we have been wrong-footed. For example, having so carefully staffed and debated teaching strategies for the lower ability boys' groups, we were taken by surprise when the vanguard year reached Year 9 and it was the boys' *top* set that proved to be the problem.

The 'wait and see' parents now appear to have made up their minds. We have been receiving a regular stream of requests to transfer pupils to our school. The first cohort has now just reached Year 10. Although that year group is still the smallest in the school, after appeals Years 9, 8 and 7 are full and with waiting lists for places. The school is routinely enjoying some 500 applications from Year 6 each year. We are convinced that this alone justifies what we are doing. We are not simply 'just another' of six competent comprehensives in Brentwood, but a school with a unique flavour that is not only extending the choice available to local parents, but also extending that choice in a way that the public obviously wants.

Parents, like teachers, feel 'in their bones' that *both* sexes will benefit from an arrangement such as ours. But is there objective proof? Of course, the big test will come with the first GCSE results in 1999 (although this vanguard year is anything but typical of the school). Obviously, we have been monitoring the effect of what we are doing internally. One fact to emerge from our own statistics is particularly interesting. The impression has remained amongst some of the more sceptical that the girls are romping ahead in their quiet, well-ordered way. However, analysis of school examination scores and the 1997 KS3 SAT results has revealed that, despite their more active approach and their noisier classroom behaviour, the boys have equalled the girls. In some cases, boys have surpassed their levels of achievement, *even though they obtained lower scores in the CAT tests that they took in the Lower School.*

Outcomes and returns

Our initiative is still young. We do not have all the answers, but we have certainly raised some questions. The research has undoubtedly made us all argue amongst ourselves and re-evaluate our teaching techniques. This alone must have had a knock-on, beneficial effect for all our pupils.

The Gender Working Party has a very prominent role within the School. The group promotes and guides research, suggests cross-curricular strategies, collates and debates data. It ensures that good practice is disseminated across the School and successful strategies in one area are available for discussion and analysis in another. Several staff meetings have been given over to the issue and specialists, such as Patricia Murphy of the Open University, have led INSET sessions for us. Departments have argued through a subject-specific gender policy for themselves. Some have developed sophisticated policies picking up on issues of self-esteem and leadership in girls' groups and discipline in boys'. The school has required at least an annual adjustment to departmental schemes of work as the vanguard year has gone through. Some, like Mathematics, have declared an intention to offer girls and boys identical subject matter. Others are tailoring what they teach according to gender.

The English Department has gathered literature for a 'girls' reading box' and a 'boys' reading box' with, naturally, some overlap. In Information Technology, boys' groups start learning about spreadsheets with an example of the football league offering a familiar context to tackle a new concept, before moving to a monetary example, and then a clothing store stock example. Girls' groups start with the fashion store stock – a motivating and reassuring context for a new concept – then money and then a sports league. Some teacher colleagues would baulk at this manipulation of gender stereotypes, but others see it as simply a means of differentiation enabling both boys and girls to feel confident with the variety of applications of spreadsheets. If differentiation is to mean anything, it surely should not ignore the differences that an individual's gender makes. Boys and girls *do* learn differently. We must accommodate their different needs within the classroom. Even at the simplest level, boys must be led to appreciate the importance of presentation, girls must accompany presentation with depth of understanding; boys must think before they speak, girls must take risks and offer an answer.

Our students have been tracked by SCITT trainees and the Chair of the Governors' Curriculum Committee, herself a teacher, in order to glean an objective perspective of what is happening in the classroom. We have filmed the same lesson given by the same teacher to a boys' and then a girls' class. It is quite clear that we are treating the boys' and girls' groups differently – even when we try not to! Yet I would contend that we automatically adjust our delivery style and, to a certain extent, our material to cater for the prevailing characteristic of *any* group in front of us, whether mixed or single sex.

From staff attendance at training courses on the subject of gender, it is interesting to note that much research has been undertaken into the different academic performance of boys and girls. However, few examples like Shenfield exist to provide evidence and example of the way the sexes perform without the classroom influence of each other's presence. Part of our difficulty is that we are breaking new ground. Many people seem to be demanding '*the* answer' to an issue for which no one blueprint exists. As a school, we are building up experience and finding out the full implications of what we have done as we go. The gender debate is a vehicle for an enforced review of classroom practice by even the most experienced on our staff. We have joined together, NQTs and senior teachers, trainees and management in a fundamental pedagogic debate.

Despite our teething problems, it is significant that our OFSTED report in 1997 greeted the issue of our initiative with complete silence. Perhaps there are no boxes to tick for this one, although I am sure they would have criticised the model under some general curriculum or management heading if they thought it was not working. The School's position of building up experience and finding out as we go, was and is an honourable one. It could not have been any other way with, at the outset, so few staff with single-sex teaching experience. Conceivably, the staff development spin-off is the single most important return for us. As John Fairhurst said in his inaugural speech to staff in April 1995: 'Develop the staff – develop the school!'

Acknowledgements

I wish to acknowledge formally the work of Dr Peter Osborne and John Fairhurst BSc in implementing the Shenfield High School initiative and to record my appreciation for their assistance in writing this article.

10

Co-education, boys, girls and achievement

Brian Matthews

The debate on whether or not the single-sex or co-educational school should predominate has been with us a long time. In the past, one of the main arguments for single-sex schools was that boys and girls had different roles and so required different education. Recently, the arguments have focused primarily on 'achievement', though this has actually been restricted to *academic* achievement. This emphasis on academic performance as a reason for separating boys and girls has two drawbacks. Firstly, it ignores recent research on the importance of 'emotional intelligence' and how the development of the whole person contributes to cognitive development. Secondly, it undervalues improving relationships and maturity as educational aims. Many people argue that the social aspects of education are very important and yet are constantly under-valued, despite it being clear that an improvement in 'emotional intelligence' should contribute to an increase in communication skills and hence, possibly, an increased understanding between the sexes.

What we have had is a schooling that has berated the 'under-achievement' by girls; now, we are getting a change in emphasis that focuses on *boys'* 'under-achievement'. What we really require is a pedagogy that moves away from this see-saw where first girls are focused on, and then boys. We need one that recognises that to achieve equality, girls' and boys' achievements have to be seen *together*. This implies that co-education is required, for as Keddie (1971, 133) showed many years ago, separation in an educational context, even in the same school, results in different curricula. Also, recent debates on equality need to be taken into account.

Equality and equity

There have been many discussions on the meaning of 'equality' (Turner, 1986; Gipps and Murphy, 1994, 7). At the core of these debates has been the concept of distribution, where 'equality' meant sharing out opportunities or resources. Young (1990), in a discussion of the meanings of social justice, has questioned equality and what she calls the 'distributive paradigm'. She argues for the concept of equity which recognises there are different forms of oppression (e.g. sexual and racial), that these experiences give rise to different concepts of justice, and that their viewpoints need to be expressed. Young (1990) and Yateman (1994) argue that while distribution may be important, an essential component of equity is that people's voices can be heard and account taken of them. They argue for an adequate *representation of identities*, rather than a redistribution of resources. In this context, 'resources' is often synonymous with 'finance'. Troyna and Vincent (1995) apply these ideas to the educational context and argue for greater diversity and levels of participation.

If these ideas are applied to the classroom, it means providing opportunities for pupils to give voice to their feelings and emotions, while ensuring an even distribution of time for talking and listening to each other in order to have an adequate representation of their identity and to affirm difference. Further, their viewpoints need to be taken into account, e.g. in group work.

These two strands – the importance of social development and voices of representation – can be brought together. For example, it is generally accepted that there are insufficient pupils, and especially girls, taking up science as a career. It could be more effective to have boys and girls communicating so that they can represent their identities, girls showing that, within a 'femininity', they can be good at physics and chemistry, and boys at biology. Together, they can discuss such issues so that social development, learning and identity can be made explicit and, thus, changed. It is then more likely that any problem will be seen as a whole – not as a boys' or girls' – problem. Boys and girls could each study their positive and negative contributions to learning and identity. Then, not only may their academic performance be similar, but also they may be more likely to continue with the subjects together. The usual approaches have been to make science more interesting to girls by, for example, making the subject more relevant. The focus has been on raising academic standards. This has been achieved, but still girls and boys take up the sciences differentially. Part of the reason for girls being influenced by arts subjects and biology, and boys by the physical sciences, is social and gender constructions. While it is true that schools have tackled sexism, this has often been done in largely different contexts.

Raising the standards that matter: the need for co-education

A primary aim for schools should be to provide an interesting and stimulating environment where pupils learn to question, think, and develop emotionally, physically and intellectually. To progress to a world in which everyone has more freedom and choice, education should have a full commitment to social and emotional development. Some people have argued that single-sex schools are a better environment for girls' learning (Shaw, 1995; Deem, 1984; Mahony, 1985). One basis of these arguments has been that girls are free from the distractions and unwelcome attentions of boys. Also, certain boys often take more teacher time and resources, so girls can be marginalised, which will reflect on their academic performance (Stanworth, 1981). Flaws in these arguments have been pointed out (Kenway and Willis, 1986; Willis and Kenway, 1986), but I believe that the debate is still too narrow (Russell, 1993; Matthews, 1996, 18). In brief, in order to challenge sexism in the long term, an understanding of the psychological and sociological processes that reproduce and maintain sexist attitudes is required. I will focus on these processes and argue the case for co-educational schools being more likely to offer a better environment than single-sex schools for engendering change that could raise 'achievement' in a broader sense than just the academic.

Masculinity and femininity as processes

Most concepts can only be understood in relation to other concepts. For example, the concept of 'town' requires an understanding of 'country'; the contrast between the two is essential for meaning. Similarly, biologically defined 'female' and 'male' have no meaning by themselves, but only in relation to each other.

In particular, 'masculinity' and 'femininity' are social constructions that can have meaning only in tandem. Some people argue, or imply, that masculinity and femininity are based in biology, and are fixed. I would argue that this is a misconception, because femininity and masculinity are actually processes. By this, I mean that we learn what it means to be masculine or feminine through the ways that we interact with people of the same and other sex. In a sense, we are our interactions, and these are often comparative (e.g. 'girls cry' implies 'boys don't'). It is through these interactions and experiences that we come to define ourselves, and these understandings change with time. Hence, masculinity and femininity are processes that are learnt, negotiated, changed and forged. They have to be worked out in a quite different way to learning what a physical object, like a tennis racket, is. To learn what femininity and masculinity are 'from a distance'- for example, in a single-sex environment – *implies* that they are fixed, like biological sex, and are not processes, let alone that they are largely social and emotional. Of course, it is possible to learn 'at a distance', but what is learnt is limited and likely to be distorted. As well as this, the way learning occurs, and what is learnt, are not separate. The methods of learning carry their own hidden curriculum.

There is a powerful body of opinion that suggests that when babies are born they have to learn what it means to be male or female (Chodorow, 1978; Head, 1997, 42). Studies have shown that difficulties arise when the female is predominantly responsible for child-rearing and the male is often absent (Dinnerstein, 1976; Chodorow, 1978). As a result, for both girls and boys, the concept of 'masculinity' can be difficult to work out and can easily become defined largely around 'not-female'.

This emphasises the differences and more easily leads to females and males being seen as opposites. The longer this process continues, and the fewer social interactions take place between the sexes, then the more dichotomous the formulation can become. Because the problems of children learning that they are separate individuals are associated with the female nurturer, it is easier to see the absent male as more objective and active in the world, and more powerful (Chodorow, 1978). Hence the more the sexes are separated, the more these processes are reinforced, and the more difficult it becomes for children to work out a realistic and equality-based view of masculinity and femininity. This separation also strongly implies that femininity and masculinity are based in biology – if for no other reason than that you cannot teach processes 'at a distance'. The separation of the sexes, at all ages, reinforces stereotypical ideas and so makes it more difficult to relate to the complementary sex.[1]

As children grow up, and as adults, we use 'fantasy' and 'phantasy' to help us understand and cope with the world. *Fantasy* is when a person uses his/her imagination to think about the world in unobtainable ways. So a teacher may fantasise that the worst class in the school will obey every command and learn like there was no tomorrow! With fantasy one is aware that one is removed from reality, but it can help both cope with and explore reality. *Phantasy* has a different meaning; it is when we are not conscious that fantasy is being used, and it is incorporated into beliefs about reality (Guntrip, 1969; Scharff, 1995, 321). So, for example, much of the racism in the 19th century that was used to 'justify' colonialism was based on phantasy of what it was genuinely believed that other races were like: indolent, sexual, and not capable of informed decisions (Fryer, 1984).

To work out what is meant by 'femininity' or 'masculinity' is very difficult for the child. The mother is usually around and so it is easier to learn through experience an idea of femininity, for both girls and boys. However, especially in the case of the absent/working father, 'masculinity' is more difficult to formulate and speculations are involved. All speculations are phantasy-laden, but if males are around to interact with, then the phantasy can possibly be made explicit and fantasy can be checked. The distorted images, often fantasy, on the television or in films, provide information for concepts to be built up. A reality emerges that is a mixture of phantasy and experience-based learning. The more separated the sexes, the more fertile is the ground for phantasy. The images that emerge can easily be the haven for sexist interpretations, the often-absent male becoming defined as not-female. From this, 'masculinity' can easily emerge in the female (and male) imagination as the active romantic/provider. Also, since the man is less involved in the complexities of the child learning to become a separate person, 'masculinity' can be seen as more 'non-emotional and objective'. In contrast, the mother is closely involved in emotional conflicts with the child, so 'femininity' can often be associated with over-emotionality and subjectiveness. One part of countering these images is to ensure young people spend time together in constructive ways and both parents take an active part in child-rearing.

For sexism to be preserved, it is essential that the sexes be seen as inherently different. Sometimes these differences are attributed to biology, and sometimes to social constructions, and it is this I wish to discuss now.

Social construction

I believe that single-sex schools are structurally sexist, and I want to explore this through an analogy. Suppose a group of workers in a factory were called to a meeting. The factory owner explained that (s)he had measured everyone's production and found that, on average, the men did 15 per cent more work than the women. As a result (s)he was going to pay the men 15 per cent more. No matter how the owner tried to justify the action, clearly this is a sexist policy. The only way such a pay differential could be 'justified' would have been if every man performed 15 per cent better than each woman. There would actually have been considerable overlap of output between men and women.

I want to emphasise that the moment the decision was made to separate out the men and the women it became sexist, and inherently biologically determinist. The factory owner may have argued that (s)he was not being determinist, and it was just that, because of the way men and women were brought up, men were better at doing the job. As much as (s)he was against this upbringing, (s)he needed to make a profit. Here the owner could claim to be a social constructionist, but clearly is not. If (s)he were, the action would have been quite different. What would have been emphasised would be the overlap and it would be stressed that women and men can have the same productivity. Efforts would then have been made to improve *everyone's* output and the assumption been one of equality, as I have defined it above. Also, any differential in pay would have been on individual performance, and so included both men and women, and they would not have been separated on the basis of biology.

This, I believe, is a parallel in schools. Single-sex schools are inherently based on biologically determinist principles and are structurally sexist because they separate people on the grounds of biological sex alone, in a similar way to the example above on pay. With schools, the situation is much more complex with many more factors involved, although the principle is the same. If we do believe in social constructionism and equality, then to separate boys and girls makes little sense. Since there is always a greater overlap on any factor between the abilities of girls and boys, to separate them on any one factor is discriminatory in practice and also reductionist. The more factors taken into account, the less there can be a justification for separation. In saying this, I accept that girls can lose out because some boys dominate the classroom, take teacher time and do not co-operate, although I would question whether the situation is as clear cut as presented by some analysts (e.g. Spender and Sarah, 1980; Deem, 1984). I fully accept that any moves to co-educational schools must confront these issues (Matthews, 1994 and 1996), but still maintain that co-educational schools are the best institutional way of tackling sexism in the long term.

Single-sex schools imply many things, but here I focus on two.

1. Sex is the major factor on which differences are based, rather than culture, class or any other variable. There are numerous ways in which people can experience discrimination, of which sexism is only one. For example, Arnot outlines the complexity of class and gender issues and indicates how a focus on single-sex schooling can support class distinctions (Arnot, 1983). I argue that all forms of discrimination have to be tackled together. This is not to say that racism, sexism or classism etc. are the same, for indeed they are not, as priorities and interests will vary from person to person. As well as this, to separate people on the basis of sex is to ignore sexuality and to lump together heterosexuals, bisexuals, gays and lesbians.

The arguments about how to combat discriminations are about the processes of liberation and domination and include the development of self-esteem, self-definition and co-operation. Also, since the 'self' can have a mature meaning only in relationship to others, *combined with an acceptance of differences*, sexism, racism and other discriminations have to be tackled jointly. To focus on one hinders this understanding. So to argue for single-sex schools, which prioritises sex, is to distort movement towards liberation for all.

2. Biology is the determining factor. In schools, we do not separate pupils in terms of eye colour: we do not see it as a significant factor. People are only separated if those who have the power see it as important. In Victorian times, single-sex schools were introduced because it was believed that women and men had quite different roles in life and so needed different education. In apartheid South Africa, black and white students were separated because of the belief that race is a major determinant. In Northern Ireland, pupils are separated on denominational grounds. In all these cases, the separation exists to support sexism, racism and religious intolerance, not to combat it. The act of separation inherently draws attention to the basis for separation and makes it important, be it due to sexism, racism or classism. Separation is accepted as a way of increasing and reinforcing racism, religious intolerance, and sexism. While these do have different roots, they have much in common psychologically. Part of the reason that separating increases intolerance and decreases understanding is that the more the 'other' is unknown, the easier it is to dump those denied parts of ourselves onto the 'other'. The 'other' becomes a greater repository the less it is defined or known, and so is easier to project onto.

Separation means that girls and boys can find it very difficult to get a realistic idea of the complementary sex. The separation not only encourages phantasy as well as fantasy, but it also makes communication difficult and so is more likely to promote an alienated and 'objectified' view of the now 'opposite' sex. The segregation implies a view of people-as-objects, rather than highlighting processes. As pupils have reported (Blishen, 1969), separation makes either boys or girls seem like a different species. It becomes hard for normal communication and relationships to grow. If a girl and a boy meet, it must be specially arranged and is fraught with tension, much of it sexual. (This is also observable in co-educational schools, especially when group work and collaborative learning in mixed groups is not common). Separation encourages the view that boys and girls do not meet to learn or to discuss, but primarily for sexual reasons. Boys tend to see girls as 'objects' of desire, mainly for sex and nurturing/mothering. Girls tend to see boys as 'objects' of desire, mainly for romance/sex and providing financial support. For both sexes, this is an unreal atmosphere that does not encourage the formation of positive relationships. In order to challenge this girls and boys must talk together in properly constructed work situations (Matthews, 1994; Matthews and Sweeney, 1997). Such talk could be part of enabling a mature sense of the complementary sex to be formed.

Separation makes it incredibly difficult for girls and boys to break out of the sexist cultural conditioning they are caught in. For true friendship to be established in relationships, knowledge of both the 'self' and 'other' is vital. This can most easily be established through a growth of knowledge based on interactions of all sorts. The more those interactions can be with a range of people – usually removed from sexual interest, but sometimes with that interest – the more realistic and sustainable will be the knowledge and the possibility, later in life, of intimate relationships of all forms. The more separated the sexes, the more out-of-focus and fantasy-based will be their view of each other. The longer the separation, the more difficult will it be for phantasy even to be recognised, let alone replaced. Research by Mary Harris (1986) confirmed Dale's (1974) work by finding that, in co-education schools, there were more other-sex friendships. Also, students were more likely to feel that the co-educational environment would help, rather than hinder, their everyday relationships with the other sex and their chances of happier relationships. Research by Kenway *et al* (1997) and Matthews and Sweeney (1997) also lends support for this view.

Hence, if we wish to emphasise the countering of sexism, the encouragement of sound relationships between all groups of people, and to stress people-knowledge, then *co-educational schools are essential*. Single-sex schools provide, inherently, fertile ground for the growth and sustenance of biological determinist ideas by ensuring the place of fantasy and phantasy, and a lack of people-knowledge between the sexes. They introduce a structural sexism and can no more be a part of countering sexism than apartheid can be a part of countering racism, public schools can be a part of countering classism, or denominational schools can be a part of countering religious bigotry. Direct communication across any socially constructed divide is essential.

So, for the reasons outlined above, mother-based child rearing and separation of the sexes can give a weak sense of the complementary sex in both girls and boys. It has been observed that many men have a fragile sense of 'self' (Kegan, 1982; Segal, 1990). Since men are often absent, both girls and boys have to form a concept of masculinity by, at least in part, making it 'not female'. This often leads to boys rejecting, and therefore devaluing, the 'feminine'. It makes 'masculinity' a difficult concept, so that boys can feel that they have constantly to achieve it (Chodorow, 1971 and 1978). Hence they can struggle to prove their masculinity, and so behave disruptively in schools, but this also makes it possible to change the comparatively fragile concept of maleness (Head, 1997, 45; Lee, 1993; Arnot, 1984). It is this fragility that can be responsible for many unwanted aspects of male behaviour. However, as I explained at the beginning, concepts of 'masculinity' and 'femininity' only make sense in tandem. Hence, the more the difficulty of working out what the 'other' is, the more this introduces an uncertainty in defining 'self'. This uncertainty can be increased if the biological reasons are believed in thus supporting sexist ideas.

No amount of telling girls how they should be equal, or how boys and girls should change, will have as much effect as confronting the processes of those changes. If one imagines girls in a single-sex school asking why they are separated from boys, the answer would probably lump all boys together. A truer answer, like '*some* boys are very disruptive' would undermine the case for separation, *especially since it is those boys and girls who can get on well together that need to be encouraged and used as role models.*

To achieve a significant liberation, we need to understand more how emotional maturity is achieved, how we achieve self-definition and self-worth, and how this links with how we see other people. It is to this I now turn.

Maturity

As we grow up, we change in the way we relate to the world. Kegan (1982) sees the child as an active meaning-maker who undergoes both differentiation and integration of meaning to make progressive syntheses. He suggests that there are certain 'evolutionary truces', the term being used to stress that processes are going on, rather than static 'stages'.

In order to mature, we have to realise that we are individuals who define ourselves through our relationships with others, and are responsible for our own states of mind and decisions. Adolescence is an important time and involves significant changes, particularly because our understanding of sexual relationships changes so much. Also, the adolescent matures and becomes able to co-ordinate different points of view and feelings. True intimacy in work and love becomes more possible when one is largely a coherent individual, able to see others as such, and to empathise with others. One is able to see that people (and organisations) are not closed systems, but are defined by the relationship between them. This is a central realisation that one's self-identity, and maleness or femaleness, is fashioned primarily through one's relationships with others, and is thus social.

We can see that to encourage maturity in girls and boys, conditions are required that generate empathy and the realisation of interconnectedness, while promoting individuality. Being together can provide examples and interactions that will help each to move on and mature. A realisation that self-worth should be based on both inclusion and differentiation helps emotional development. The point is that each sex is limited to the extent it denies one side, rather than each being balanced. 'The struggle of the sexes to know each other, to see each other, and to communicate deeply... may rest in the capacity of men and women to learn the universal language they share...the dialectical context in which these two poles are joined' (Kegan, 1982, 209-10). As

Tannen (1990) has indicated, if each person has the psychological attributes that supposedly belong to the other sex, there is a tendency to have greater flexibility, better social relations and personal happiness. In this struggle to communicate, there is more chance of psychological androgyny, if for no other reason than that separation is likely to reinforce splitting and projection.

Splitting and projection

Splitting and projection are psychological processes that occur all the time (Klein, 1988; Sandler, 1987). We can have aspects of our personality, feelings or wishes that we do not like, or cannot face up to. These aspects can be denied, and projected onto others. We can then attack this projection and feel that we have 'dealt with it'. For example, a macho man can be unable to be in contact with his passive 'feminine' side, and so project it onto homosexuals. These he will attack, both as a defence against recognising it in himself, and feeling that by attacking it he has combated it.

Since adolescence involves forging new meaning about 'femaleness' and 'maleness', the processes of denial of parts of oneself (splitting) and locating this part in someone else (projection) in this area can be increased (Kenway et al, 1997). Hence, boys can deny their passive, emotional and nurturing sides and locate these in girls in order to confirm their 'masculinity'. Meanwhile, girls project their aggressive, objective and hard sides onto boys in order to confirm their 'femininity'. In the co-educational environment, provided suitable communication takes place, these splitting and projection processes can be checked, worked on, and challenged in constructive ways that can never be done in single-sex schools. In one's search for sexual identity, 'certainties' are very useful – hence the power of accepting stereotypes. To challenge such certainties requires a lot of psychological and emotional energy, and it is valuable to be confronted with, for example, the many passive boys and assertive girls who refute the projection at the same time as it is being constructed.

Relying on uninspected 'certainties' (Kegan, 1982) can stunt the maturing processes. Parts of the self can be projected onto others, which thereby impoverishes and curtails the development of self because the required exploration of differences is truncated (White, 1992). Maturing is weakened by oversimplification. The 'certainties' can also help see others as need-objects rather than maturing to seeing that needs are relative and that people are defined through processes and the relationship between them.

The single-sex environment is important in that it provides group solidarity and enables cathartic talk. If unchecked, however, it can be very negative. Male group solidarity and projection processes enable 'stereotypical-females' to become the repository for society's ills. Female teachers who enter this environment soon become painfully aware of this, and some boys confirm their 'masculinity' by displaying their lack of emotion and aggressiveness. As we can see, the argument that male teachers should tackle this problem in all-male schools is quite untenable, for the longer the separation the more strongly will be the internalisations of projection and splitting, and the attendant 'monocultural' responses. Exactly the same processes can go on in girls' schools, and it is just as important for them to explore differences and mature. The girls can confirm their 'femininity' when a male teacher enters the environment by displaying their passivity and emotional concern. Hence, some become 'unable' to do tasks – like putting on an electric plug – and expect the man to do it, and give more weight to male utterances. The suppression of attitudes has a negative effect. The female sees the man as 'taking over the situation' and not giving her credit for her ability. The male sees the woman not being able, and expecting him to do the work. Attitudes can be confirmed with mutual resentment. In each case, self-esteem can be maintained and gender roles reinforced in a way that leaves them uninspected.

It is possible to challenge both of these mutually destructive situations, although the aggression of males is more visible and condemned. The point is that because 'femininity' and 'masculinity' are processes, and the definition of one is inseparable from the other, synchronous changes can occur. These changes have to be tackled in tandem, in that the more that girls and boys go through the processes together, the greater the likelihood of change. As Isabel Menzies Lyth (1989) has shown, the psychological processes are integral with sociological ones. The way we interact is inseparable from both the social beliefs brought to any situation and the defence mechanisms, like splitting and projection, because what is projected, or denied, is influenced by social values.

One aspect for decreasing sexism is for youngsters to learn that gender roles are relative, and that girls and boys can have an empathy and compassion for each other. Adolescence is a crucial period where, partly because of physical maturation, understandings and meanings of many things change. We should help adolescents to mature emotionally and intellectually through this period, which can best be done by facing up to the difficulties and not running away from them. I agree that co-educational schools will probably be more difficult places to teach in than single-sex schools because of those challenges, but that is not a reason against them. A wide variety of experiences are required to develop emotionally and to mature. Because of present socialisations girls and boys have different needs, and boys especially need to express their emotions more; but so do girls, for both sexes find it difficult to talk about important matters, even though girls are better at it than boys.

It seems to me that we all need to understand the complexity of living and the joy, fun and intimacy that relationships and mutuality of understanding can bring. However, this can only be accomplished through people meeting each other as people, and not through the lens of stereotypes. The separation of boys and girls into single-sex schools carries a powerful hidden message: that behaviour is largely genetically determined and is fixed.

Moving forward

We can focus primarily on either a long term or a short term approach to the issue of achievement in schools. The short term, in my view, is to look at schools and argue that by making sure girls achieve well, they will have greater self-esteem and be able to take up careers that place them at the top of society. I have no disagreement with this aim. However, I think it is severely limited. In the long term, we must enable boys and girls to understand each other and their differences, while maintaining academic achievement. This will enable boys and girls to want to work together at all levels in society, increase their self-esteem and so help prevent the circle of sexism continuing. This means placing social aspects of achievement at least as high as the cognitive ones. Then schools, and in particular co-education, can contribute to tackling sexism and development of the 'self'.

However, for co-education to do this, it is not sufficient just to put boys and girls together. It is also necessary to have strategies that will tackle emotional and cognitive factors. Most research still tends to look at girls' progress or boys' underachievement, the latter being a growing interest. There is very little research on boys and girls *working co-operatively* in secondary schools to raise achievement. A project I am involved in aims to treat these issues (Matthews, 1994; Matthews and Sweeney, 1997).

CASE STUDY

Helping pupils learn science in a co-educational setting

The focus of the project is on group work and finding ways of enabling pupils to discuss their *learning* of science, and how they *feel* about working a) in the group, and b) about their feelings towards science. The research involved three secondary (11-16) schools and one post-16 college.

The pupils engaged in group work while learning the normal science curriculum and were monitored to see how each person had contributed to the task. They had been told that both listening and talking skills were regarded as important (Matthews, 1994). The teacher formed the groups so that there were two girls and two boys in each group. A pupil-observer who watched a group of four pupils involved in a discussion of a science topic, and filled in a chart while the pupils talked, carried out external monitoring. At the end of the discussion, each of the four members of the group were required to estimate, without consulting anyone, how well they and the other three in the group had performed. The criteria comprised the amount of talking listening, interrupting, being supportive and learning taking place. Space for any additional comments was included. This stage was intended to make visible any gap between what one thinks happened, and what others think happened, so that consciousness might be raised. The observer wrote down any comments considered relevant.

The pupil-observer then discussed the results with the group in order to bring attention to the different ways the pupils had interpreted the talk, and to raise questions about the patterns of talk. In general, it was useful for the observer to get the members of the group to go over their estimates and to see the extent to which they correlated. This was to make evident any gap between what each member who talked thought had transpired and what the observer had found. The purpose here was to promote a discussion on how people felt about the processes of learning, and to have some evidence on which to base the debate.

The discussion assessment sheets filled by the observers (for pupils aged 12 and 13) showed that in general the amount of speech was distributed fairly evenly between girls and boys. The extent of talking between boys and girls was much more balanced than other studies have indicated. For example, some studies have indicated that the boys dominate, taking up to two thirds of the time (Stanworth, 1981; Spender and Sarah, 1988; Holden, 1993). This suggests that the monitoring and feedback discussions are having a beneficial effect.

In this chapter, it is not possible to detail the research and its results. The techniques are now well developed and the indications are that when group work is *combined with monitoring and feedback*, then:

• the quantity of talk between boys and girls becomes more balanced

• the boys and girls express improved attitudes to group work

• the pupils feel that they get on, and understand each other better, as they do more group work and have feedback discussions

• the pupils say that they find science more social and interesting.

Here are some quotations from the pupils:

Group work has definitely made relationships better with the other sex. It has made me feel better to talk to them... they'll listen to me and respect me... you get to know them better... I have experienced less sexism. [Female, Bengali]

It has made me feel more confident to work with other girls... my respect for them has grown. [Male, Bengali]

Doing group work helps you understand the people you are working with. [Female, Indian]

Work is more interesting because you can talk about your feelings and someone else's. [Female, British]

I do get on better with the others as we do more group work. [Male, African]

We got on well, with no differences with the girls or race, and get better as we do more. [Male, Indian]

Yes, because you get to meet different people and get to know them and sometimes people have a lot more in common but they don't know it. [Male, White]

This indicates that group work, when combined with monitoring and feed-back discussions, could lead to a development of pupils' attitudes to, and understanding of, each other (emotional intelligence) and an increase in positive attitudes to science. It also offers support for co-educational schools as a way of promoting understanding between the sexes. A fuller discussion of the findings, but focusing more on intercultural attitudes, is published in Matthews and Sweeney, 1997.

Some people are engaged in research that links with co-education, even though it does not have as its central aim the improvement of boys and girls learning together. For example, there is the work by Cowie *et al* (1994), on co-operative group work in the multi-ethnic classroom, and the Newham Conflict and Change Project, which seeks to help young people resolve their conflicts together. These projects are not aimed specifically at gender relationships, but are an integral part of it. They point to the lack of 'emotional literacy' in schools and say how important its development is in helping children (Cowie *et al*, 1994; Musgrave, 1997). Part of the latter project emphasises mediation. The importance of pupils with a wide diversity of backgrounds meeting and interacting is stressed, since this is seen as an integral part of pupils understanding each other, being more flexible and integrated into the learning situation (Cohen, 1996). In America there is a large organisation, the Collaborative for Social and Emotional Learning (CASEL, 1997), which promotes and argues for the importance of the development of emotional intelligence. All this work gives indirect support for educating boys and girls together in order to improve all aspects of learning, including the cognitive.

Conclusion

Debates on the purpose of education will continue for ever. There is one viewpoint that argues for a concentration on academic achievement, to the exclusion of many other factors, like critical thinking, being able to cope with contradictions and uncertainty, and the development of the whole social person. At present, this camp is in the ascendant and education in Britain is in a negative grip: that of 'academic achievement'. This is a restricted definition of achievement that is leading to a focus on boys and single-sex environments. This is, at least in part, because single-sex girls schools that draw on middle and upper class pupils achieve well academically.

In contrast, especially in America but also in Britain, an increasing number of people are lobbying for a much wider of range of aims to be central to education. The formation of the group *Antidote*, arguing for the promotion of emotional literacy in schools, is one such indication. Such an emphasis seems sensible, especially given that gender roles in society are changing and the importance of communication in all sorts of relationships is constantly stressed. For example, research for British Telecom has shown how a lack of social skills holds adolescents back in all sorts of ways (Catan, 1996). The development of social and emotional skills requires flexibility, ability to deal with ambiguities and development of people who can think critically and reflectively. This makes it all the more disturbing that schools, largely because of government emphasis, are so much in the grip of the measurable, the certain, the predictable and, especially, the controllable. As a result, 'achievement' is confined to the academic and many vital aspects of learning are neglected. Somewhere along the line, it seems that many people have forgotten that social and emotional growth is *integral* to the development and use of cognitive abilities. Indeed, one could ask what is going on in those people's minds who wish to separate them in the first place.

We urgently need a re-defining of Britain's educational aims and of what 'achievement' means, which should result in benefits not only to boys and girls, but also to society. It is possible to encourage *both* academic achievement and the ability of boys and girls to know, understand and empathise with each other. These developments will help improve emotional and cognitive literacies and will benefit all, especially in the long term. The necessary changes can be done well in the co-educational setting, provided that social development is placed high on the educational agenda.

Note

1. Describing women and men as 'opposites' reinforces sexism. The term 'opposite' reinforces discrimination and makes equal opportunities more difficult. The reason for this is that it *implies* that whatever one's gender is, the other is not. So if women are nurturers, men are not. If men are lively, women are passive. I believe that an essential part of combating sexism is for male and female to be seen as complementary, although even this word does not reinforce the similarities enough. Women and men are complementary in terms of biology and reproduction.

References

Arnot M (1984): How Shall We Educate Our Sons? In Deem R: *Co-education Reconsidered*. Buckingham, Open University Press.

Arnot M (1983): A Cloud over Co-education: An Analysis of the Forms of Transmission of Class and Gender. In Walker S and Barton L (Eds): *Gender, Class and Education*. London: Falmer Press.

Blishen E (1969): *The School That I'd Like*. Harmondsworth, Penguin.

CASEL (1997): *Social and Emotional Guidelines for Educators*. Chicago, Collaborative for Social and Emotional Learning.

Catan L, Dennison C and Coleman J (1996): *Getting Through: Effective Communication in the Teenage Years*. London, BT Forum.

Chodorow N (1971): Being and Doing; a cross-cultural examination of the socialisation of males and females. In Gornick V and Noran B K (Eds): *Women in Sexist Society*. Basic Books.

Chodorow N (1978): *The Reproduction of Mothering: Psychoanalysis and the Sociology of Gender*. University of California Press.

Cowie H, Smith P, Boulton M and Laver R: (1994): *Cooperation in the Multi-Ethnic Classroom*. London, Fulton.

Dale R R (1974): *Mixed or Single-sex School? Volume 2 (Some social aspects) Volume 3 (Attainment, attitudes and overview)*. London, Routledge and Kegan Paul.

Deem R (Ed) (1984): *Co-education Reconsidered*. Buckingham, Open University Press.

Dinnerstein D (1976): *The Rocking of the Cradle, and the Ruling of the World.* New York, Harper and Row.

Fryer P (1984): *Staying Power. The History of Black People in Britain.* London, Pluto Press.

Gipps C and Murphy P (1994): *A Fair Test?* Buckingham, Open University Press.

Guntrip H (1969): *Schizoid Phenomena, Object Relations and the Self.* New York, International Universities Press.

Harris M (1986): Coeducation and Sex Roles. *Australian Journal of Education*, 30 (2), 117-31.

Head J (1997): *Working with Adolescents: Constructing Identity.* London, Falmer Press.

Holden C (1993): Giving Girls a Chance: patterns of talk in co-operative group work. *Gender and Education*, 5 (2), 179-189.

Keddie N (1971): Classroom Knowledge. In Young M F D: *Knowledge and Control.* London, Macmillan.

Kegan R (1982): *The Evolving Self.* Harvard, Harvard University Press.

Kenway J and Willis S (1986): Feminist Single-Sex Educational Strategies: Some Theoretical Flaws and Practical Fallacies. *Discourse*, 7 (1), 1-30.

Kenway J and Willis S with Blackmore J and Rennie L (1997): Are boys victims of feminism in schools? Some answers from Australia. *International Journal of Inclusive Education*, 1 (1), 19-35.

Klein M (1988): *Envy and Gratitude and other works, 1946-1963.* London, Virago.

Lee C (1993): *Talking Tough. The fight for masculinity.* London, Arrow.

Lyth M I (1989): *The Dynamics of the Social, Volume 2.* London, Free Association Books.

Mahony P (1985): *Schools for Boys?* London, Hutchinson.

Matthews B (1994): Promoting Equal Opportunities: Starting Girls and Boys Communicating. *Journal of Teacher Development*, 3 (3), 149-158.

Matthews B (1996): Peacemakers in the battle of the sexes. *Times Educational Supplement.* 17/5/96, 18.

Matthews B and Sweeney J (1997): Collaboration in the science classroom to tackle racism and sexism. *Multicultural Teaching*, 15 (3), 33-36.

Musgrave R (1998): *Creative Conflict Resolution. A workshop approach in schools.* In press.

Russell J (1993): Going Co-ed in the 90s and the Search for Core Values: Valuing the Feminine, Finding the Good. *Feminist Teacher*, 7 (3), 11-20.

Sandler J (Ed) (1987): *Projection, Identification, Projective Identification.* Connecticut, International Universities Press.

Scharff D (1995): *Object Relations Theory and Practice.* London, Aronson.

Segal L (1990): *Slow Motion. Changing Masculinities, Changing Men.* London, Virago.

Shaw J (1995): *Education, Gender and Anxiety.* London, Taylor and Francis.

Stanworth M (1981): *Gender and Schooling: A study of sexual divisions in the classroom.* London, Women's Research and Resources Centre Publications.

Tannen D (1990): *You Just Don't Understand. Women and Men in Conversation.* London, Virago.

Troyna B and Vincent C (1995): The Discourses of Social Justice in Education. *Discourse*, 16 (2), 149-166.

Turner B (1986): *Equality.* London, Tavistock Publications.

White J (1992): *Adolescence and Education in the 1990s.* London, City University.

Willis S and Kenway J (1986): On overcoming Sexism in Schooling: To Marginalize or Mainstream. *Australian Journal of Education*, 30 (2), 132-49.

Yeatman A (1994): *Postmodern Revisionings of the Political.* London, Routledge.

Young I (1990): *Justice and the Politics of Difference.* New Jersey, Princeton University Press.

11

Improvement through partnership
How Kirklees LEA, schools and higher education worked together to boost boys' performance

Wendy Bradford

Partnership in school

Generating school improvement to raise boys' achievement requires change. The essential link between improvement and change is outlined by Reynolds, who defines improvement as 'a distinctive approach to educational change that enhances student outcomes as well as strengthening the school's capacity for managing change' (Reynolds in Hopkins *et al.*, 1994, 104). Change is uncomfortable and involves 'hearts and minds'. Whilst academic debate and well-crafted argument might convince the mind, a convincing emotional appeal will still be necessary to fuel change. The changes may appear to be structural, but they are also fundamentally personal.

Change is not just about the creation of new policies and pro-cedures to implement external mandates. It is also about the development of personal strategies by individuals to respond to, and seek to influence the impact of structural and cultural change:

personal change as much as organisational change. (Bennett *et al.,* 1992, 2)

This chapter describes a project undertaken by Kirklees LEA, in partnership with local schools and Huddersfield University, to improve boys' under-performance between the ages of 11 and 16. There are two ways of viewing the kind of change that is necessary in an initiative such as this. It could be argued that boys themselves, or at least *some* boys, must begin to do some things differently; for example, they must spend longer on their homework, they must choose friends who want to work hard. It is, however, unlikely that boys will change their behaviour with respect to learning until there are related changes in the teaching they experience, the expectations they internalise and the targets they are encouraged to set. 'Things' have to be done differently in the classroom and in the school.

So, any exercise in raising boys' achievement must focus on teaching strategies used in the classroom, methods of behaviour management and approaches to praise and feedback used in the school. Such a focus should also affect the nature and type of support a school receives from 'outside', in this case in the form, first, of LEA support, in generating and channelling appropriate resources, support for management and staff development and so forth. Second, the support of higher education is useful in reflective practice and facilitating the establishment of academic networking. Thirdly, it may involve changing the way boys work at home, with its matched impact on how parents work with their children, and how a school, or a network of schools within an LEA, promotes these ideas to parents.

Effective change should, therefore, involve linking the practices of individual students in the classroom with the nature of management and leadership in the school. More broadly, it should involve the relationship of a single school to a wider network of schools, within the framework of support offered by the LEA and by Higher Education.

The type of school management that is seen as best able to generate and sustain educational change is one that is often referred to as 'democratic' or 'collegial'. These models offer an essentially participatory view of school management, one based on 'interactive professionalism' (Fullan and Hargreaves, 1992, 4). There is, of course, nothing *necessarily* effective about such management styles. A number of writers (Fullan and Hargreaves, 1992; Frith and Mahony, 1994; Barber, 1996) caution against the ineffective and superficial appeal to collegiality for its own sake. Collaboration, on its own, could achieve nothing. In its weakest form, it may get no further than sharing personal experiences, without any attempt being made to question or extend the practices that underpinned these experiences. Pseudo-collegiality can lead to the reduction of creativity through producing 'group-think', a confirmation of existing weaknesses within the status quo and a move to what Frith and Mahony refer to, in a slightly different context, as 'an equality of awfulness' (1994, 104). Effective collaboration will be uncomfortable, since 'in collaborative cultures, failure and uncertainty are not protected and defended... teachers do not waste time and energy covering their backs here' (Fullan and Hargreaves, 1994, 66).

Effective collaboration must eliminate the culture through which teachers feel obliged to work alone, in a culture of *individualism*, whilst enhancing the need for *individuality*, i.e. a sense that a teacher's experience, and creative responses to that experience, will augment the whole. This, of course, presupposes the idea that teachers feel they have a creative contribution to make. It soon became clear within this project that, following years of externally imposed educational change generated by the Education Reform Act of 1988, teachers had lost confidence in their sense that they could make a difference to what happened in school. They perceived they had become the 'bit-part' players within the education system; a system that was now so tightly defined there was nothing about which to collaborate. Fullan and Hargreaves describe the sense of professional decay that can result:

> *Holding back what you know, being unconfident about what you have to offer, being reticent to seek better ways of doing things and treating teachers like they need help and have little to give are all ways in which the tradition of individualism retards progress, and keeps teaching fundamentally unsatisfying in the long run. (op. cit., 59)*

An unforeseen, though extremely positive, adjunct to the work on raising boys' achievement has been the way in which it has helped to reassert one crucial idea. It is what teachers do in the classroom, how student behaviour is managed, and how varied opportunities for effective teaching and learning are created, which will produce improved levels of attainment for all students.

One Headteacher commented that teachers involved in the project had become more professionally critical about practices they had taken for granted over a period. This change of 'mind set' was influencing all aspects of their work and not ones solely concerned with the particular strategy related to boys. A similar picture of school improvement contributing to the development of 'a learning profession' (Barber, 1996, 234) is painted by Frith and Mahony:

> *The teachers were keen to increase their own professional knowledge and understanding and their interest and confidence grew further as they shared their work with colleagues whom they knew to be interested... As the project managers we saw teachers teaching each other, learning from each other and getting really involved with each other's work. (op. cit., 105)*

As Fullan and Hargreaves note,

> *Educational reform has failed time and time again... this is because reform has either ignored teachers or oversimplified what teaching is about. Reform has failed because the focus has not been on the total school and the total teacher as these relate to the learning of students. (op. cit., 4)*

In outlining their perception of 'interactive professionalism', they see the following characteristics to be of central importance:

- teachers have more discretion in making decisions, with and for the students they know best

- teachers make these decisions through a helpful and supportive collaborative culture within the school

- teachers should be able to reflect on the 'how' of what is taught and not just the 'what'

The characteristics of immature and mature organisations

IMMATURE	MATURE
Reinforcement of the status quo, deference to experience	A belief in continuous improvement, challenging traditional assumptions
Aims and objectives not clear or differentiated	Explicit aims translated into meaningful objectives and attainable personal targets
Rigid hierarchy, work segmented by status and administrative procedures, centralised control	Self-managing, task oriented teams, minimal rules, simple decentralised structure
Top-down communication, little feed-back	Communication open, honest, direct and two-way, managers listening
Motivation by coercion	Motivation recognised, rewards in personal terms
Leadership by exhortation and dictat, inflexible style	Leadership by visible example, situational style
Decisions announced	Full consultation of all involved
Training in functional terms only, no integration	Training and development fully integrated to achieve institutional objectives
Administrative and technical delegation to middle management	Real delegation of responsibility and authority to a developed middle management
Recruitment and selection on the basis of cloning	Job and personal specifications used as part of rational selection procedures
No definition of quality	An emphasis on quality in all relationships and procedures
Deference to the authority of experience	Recognition and utilisation of skills, knowledge and qualities
Assumption of client's needs	Responsiveness to clients' perception of needs
Change perceived as a threat	Change regarded as the norm

- teachers are committed to norms of continuous improvement

- teachers are more accountable as they engage in dialogue, action and assessment of their work with other adults both in and outside their schools.

What is required, therefore, is a structure of management in the school that allows these characteristics to develop and flourish. In adapting ideas from American management theorists Kanter (1981) and Peters (1987), West-Burnham (in Davies, 1990, 106) distinguishes between immature and mature organisations, the latter being most capable of generating and sustaining improvement.

The dichotomy on page 199 would seem to suggest that the government's drive to produce school improvement through external control techniques of employing more inspectors for OFSTED, and declaring criteria concerning the 'how' of teaching, are misplaced. Instead, the focus must move into the school, indeed to the teacher and to consideration of each student, so that individuals become accountable for their performance as a prerequisite to being committed and motivated to achieve high quality outcomes.

This study does not include a detailed consideration of the management styles of senior colleagues in the secondary schools that participated in this work. One point was quite apparent, however. In schools with well-established patterns of diffused authority through different levels – where the generation of innovation from 'below' was welcomed as warmly as that generated from 'above' – there was a greater readiness to consider new issues and to incorporate them into existing agendas, without seemingly creating a feeling of 'over-load'.

The penultimate characteristic of mature/immature organisations as given above adds an interesting and important extension to the concept of collegiality: it should not stop at the level of teaching colleagues, but should embrace the motivations, attitudes and energies of students. As Frith and Mahony learned through their experiences,

> *This project reminds us that the so-called bottom-up approach, highlighted by many educators... does not start with classroom teachers, but with the pupils themselves. We have, for too long,*

'done equal opportunities' to the children rather than allowing them to participate in setting the agenda whilst working alongside them... The most successful projects were those which encouraged children to research the issues for themselves, discover their own strategies and evaluate their findings. (op. cit., 109)

It is hoped that the notion of generating change from the aspirations and preferred learning styles of students is one on which this project is grounded. It helps to explain two things. First, there is the importance attached to discovering students' attitudes to a variety of issues regarding teaching and learning (two separate surveys each covering 1,000 students were carried out). Second, the practical strategies emerging from this study which are offered as vital to issues of raising boys' achievement, give central consideration to classroom management and the various interactions of teacher and students within it.

Partnership with LEA and Higher Education

The present project involved schools working within the framework of support offered by Kirklees LEA. Through a number of contracts related to education, links had been established between the LEA and the University of Huddersfield. The present project is a further example of the benefits that can be gained through such a partnership; I am both a registered student of the University and a teacher within one of the LEA's twenty-three secondary schools.

Somekh (1994) sees that whilst collaborative research between teachers in schools and university-based researchers can be problematic, it is also beneficial and, indeed, essential:

We live in a world of action, a world in which the nature of existence is shaped by perceptions, and this strongly suggests that knowledge constructed without the active participation of practitioners can only be partial knowledge. (Somekh, 1994, 367)

In his review of work to achieve school improvement through a partnership of schools, LEA and university, Arnold (1995) notes a report produced by the Centre for Successful Schools at Keele University, which reviewed sixty such partnerships. LEAs were noted as originators of 58.3 per cent of these projects, either alone or with others; TECs and Education/Business partnerships were other major contributors. The most popular area of expected improvement was 'higher pupil attainment' (85%). From this review, Arnold noted one of the main principles for effective working:

> *Loose collaboration rather than formal structure provides the pattern for the organisation of urban education initiatives, but LEAs will remain the most important players in the game... The survey evidence shows that LEAs play an important role in improving the quality of education in urban areas. In doing so they depend less on their greatly reduced formal powers and much more on the quality of their relationships with schools or what might be called their moral authority as representative of a given city or area.* (Arnold, 1995, 11)

Insights into the essential characteristics of projects constructed to create school improvement through partnership of school, LEA and Higher Education are offered by work published under the title *Improving the Quality of Education for All* (IQEA). Conducted by the University of Cambridge Institute of Education, this involved a number of schools within LEAs over the two phases of its work. The project, which was founded on a contract between the staff of the school, the LEA and university tutors, was based on six assumptions:

- school improvement will result in enhanced outcomes for pupils and teachers

- the school culture to which the project is working will embrace collaboration and high expectations

- a key factor in improvement is the school's background and organisation, which affects its values and is strongly related to the culture

- school improvement works best when the school's priorities offer a clear and practical focus

- the management arrangements of the school, i.e. its conditions, will be worked on at the same time as the priorities the school has set itself

- through becoming linked to the management arrangements of the school, the school improvement strategy will itself become part of the school's routine practices.

Establishing a collaborative base for the Kirklees project

The value of such collaborative ventures is recognised in the recent EOC/OFSTED report, *The Gender Divide*:

> *Clusters of schools can work together to identify local or regional characteristics in the profile of achievement by both sexes. They can then work with local communities, TECs and employers to raise expectations if one sex is underperforming. Equality targets can be developed, taking account of local circumstances, to focus on raising the achievement of the under performing group, either in an area of the curriculum or in terms of a more general educational target such as post-16 participation. This could then lead to a sharing of strategies between schools and a joint evaluation of progress.* (EOC/OFSTED, 1996, 8)

The University of Huddersfield was recognised as a central partner in all submissions to the LEA and the TEC. It would be difficult to quantify the total benefits that accrue from establishing a close working link between a practitioner-researcher and colleagues within a University. Reimer and Bruce provide one view of such collaboration:

> *A school-based researcher who knows the students over extended periods of time, who understands the school setting, who knows something of the students' experiences with other teachers, who knows parents and community concerns and values, and who participates in the classroom and school culture in an integral way, brings invaluable expertise to any study. At the same time, a university-based researcher whose work demands familiarity with scholarly work on teaching and learning, who knows about research designs and publication practices, or who has the opportunity to observe many classrooms, also brings special expertise.* (1994, 213)

With all the externally-generated educational changes of recent years, particularly those produced by the 1988 Education Reform Act, it was felt that teachers were showing signs of a condition which remains officially unrecognised – IFS (Initiative Fatigue Syndrome)! It was hoped that work on the Raising Boys' Achievement project would lead colleagues in schools to generate their own patterns of change to teaching and learning strategies; change which would be manageable and sustainable and which would, therefore, become embedded in 'good practice' within school.

Something of a paradox may be apparent at this point. It is assumed that to be effective, work must include the professional expertise and insights of teachers, yet the outcome of this work may well involve recommending changes to the very practices that have been shaped by this expertise. Teachers' authority of expertise must be genuinely valued if they are to be motivated participants in the work, yet the work itself may lead to uncomfortable but necessary changes to well-established practice. As Hutchinson and Whitehouse note:

> *Only when teachers realise that their views of professional competence are prejudices which have to be tested, rather than uncritically accepted, can they begin to build a constructive critique of their social practice.* (1986, 91)

Somekh provides a rather gentler view of professional change where, rather than seeking to destroy and supplant teachers' taken-for-granted assumptions, work will add to teachers' understandings and range of strategies. She argues that:

> *The process of change is integrated with the development of new understandings of the implications of personalised action, in particular of the unintended consequences of habitual or routinised behaviour... The routines of professional practice are enriched by the intellectual challenge of research.* (1995, 343)

In a separate article, Somekh (1994) outlines how collaboration with higher education can help schools to 'unsettle' or 'dent' patterns of normative socialisation in school which may be providing a firm resistance to change. Through such collaboration,

The private world of the individual classroom is placed in the context of other classrooms, in other schools; the patterns of practice across the education system can be explored by meta-analysis of action research in many individual classrooms. Teachers and their university-based partners each play a different part in this joint enterprise... School-university collaborations appear to be able to generate the cross-classroom knowledge of trends or practice and the within-classroom practical wisdom which together enable teachers to overcome some of these systematic problems. (1994, 377-378)

Getting interested in boys

On a dull and wet Thursday night in October 1993 at the University of Huddersfield, I was asked to declare a proposal for a forthcoming MEd dissertation. It had been a gruelling day as a Head of Year 10, dealing with a seemingly endless stream of incidents involving boys, e.g. bad behaviour in lessons, fighting at morning break, rudeness to lunch-time supervisors and lack of effort with homework. So it was inevitable that the topic of boys' response to secondary schooling, in terms of attitudes to schooling and outcomes at age 16, should be a central concern.

Having chosen to study 'The progress of boys in secondary school', the early signs were far from promising. In attempting to use ERIC as the preliminary basis for a literature search, there was a vast number of references to research exploring links between gender and schooling, with well over one thousand relating to girls and only twelve to boys. In diligently pursuing the dozen references to the schooling of boys, it was clear that the life of boys in borstal, boys demonstrating special needs and boys in physical education had already caught researchers' interest. However, there was a dearth of published material about the academic progress of 'ordinary' boys in 'ordinary' schools. It certainly appeared at this stage that 'gender' meant girls.

As work progressed and secondary schools were approached to take part in a survey of student attitudes relating to aspects of schoolwork, a stronger interest in 'the boys' issue' was apparent. Colleagues from a number of schools commented that they had felt for some time that 'something needed to be done about boys'. In the case of some schools, interest had been encouraged by the publication of 'league tables' of results at GCSE. The need to have as many students as possible scoring 5 or more A*-C grades drew an eye to those unlucky students who were letting down their school by unhelpfully scoring grades D and E. Even a cursory glance at examination results showed that in most schools it was boys who were letting down the side. Some schools were also encouraged to focus on this issue through comments given in their OFSTED report. Mainly through a lack of time, enquiry had often halted at this preliminary stage of identifying a broad area of concern.

The dissertation progressed to publication in 1995 and an outline of the work was passed to the Head of the Kirklees Education Advisory Service. Interest at this level produced the beginnings of the collaborative network, as funding was forthcoming from the Kirklees and Calderdale TEC, with matched funding from the LEA. This allowed the author to be seconded for one day a week through the academic year 1995-96, with further support from the TEC allowing this to continue through 1996-97. A secondment of one day a week for two years is comparable in time to a block secondment of one school term. Using a model of secondment based on one day a week was considered to be a preferable option in placing emphasis on keeping the work moving forward. To use an analogy drawn from Athletics, school improvement must be regarded as a well-paced marathon rather than an explosive sprint, so an appropriate form of secondment was needed to facilitate desired changes.

The seventy eight days of secondment were used in a variety of ways:

Establishing and maintaining a national network of contacts relevant to the theme of Raising Boys' Achievement. Contacts were drawn from Higher Education, LEAs, schools, freelance educational consultants and authors, and a variety of government-linked organisations, such as OFSTED, HMI and the Basic Skills Agency.

Making presentations to various groups within secondary schools – curriculum teams, pastoral teams, equal opportunities groups, whole staff INSET events – in order to raise awareness of issues and to suggest a portfolio of practical strategies which could be shaped to fit the school's particular situation and needs.

Working alongside the local media partially satisfied the desire to raise awareness of the issue across the LEA's community of students and parents. Local newspapers, BBC Look North television, and local and national radio were contacted.

Working with individual secondary schools within the LEA to support identification of issues relevant to raising boys' achievement in a particular institution, with a central emphasis on generating practical strategies to address identified needs and on evaluating progress towards objectives.

Organising and leading a number of collaborative meetings within the LEA which would draw together colleagues from its 23 secondary schools working on this issue in order to share ideas, progress, obstacles, and also to maintain the momentum of the work. Through 1996-7, a funded meeting took place each term. This offered colleagues access to nationally known figures, such as Peter Downes, Madeleine Arnot and Geoff Hannan, and also, crucially, to hear what work was being undertaken by other teachers in the LEA.

Producing and marketing a resource pack in collaboration with colleagues from the Kirklees Education Advisory Service, which progressed under the working title *The Boy Done Good*, but which was eventually marketed under the heading *Raising Boys' Achievement.* A version of this paper and video pack was produced for both primary and secondary sectors and was launched at a conference attended by 200 delegates at the McAlpine Stadium in Huddersfield on 1st October 1996. The pack was advertised by the Kirklees Education Advisory Service to all primary and secondary schools within England. At the time of writing (summer 1997), over 1000 have been sold and the pack has been favourably reviewed in a number of educational publications. Feedback on this resource has been received from purchasers in Australia and the USA.

Enabling schools to survey the attitudes of their own students to various aspects of their schooling. The questionnaire ('How's It Going?' from the Kirklees *Raising Boys' Achievement* pack) was used, not only to provide data for the author's continuing academic work, but also as a way of creating interest amongst teachers in the schools concerned. Data was seen to be more relevant when it showed what 'our' students think about their progress and the educational experiences 'we' are providing for them. In order to help schools use this data as a starting-point for further discussion and action, each of the schools was provided with a report detailing the responses of their students. These were deliberately written in a reasonably lively, even colloquial, style, with an emphasis on being accessible to all colleagues within school.

One interesting insight that became apparent as the project progressed, and which may have a more general applicability to action researchers, was that it is difficult to be a 'prophet in one's own country'. Put more transparently, whilst people in 'other' schools may be keen to take note of what one has to offer, it can be more difficult in one's 'own' school. This problem revealed itself in two rather opposed ways. First, when the issue of 'boys' was mentioned, it was assumed it could be left to the author to decide what needed to be done and get things moving; after all, she was the 'expert' in this area. This, apparently, implicitly relieved others of the professional responsibility to get involved; something which was obviously necessary for the project to be able to move forward, particularly as it was rooted in the idea of modifying practice in the classroom. Second, the 'issue' and the 'personality' became so inextricably linked in people's minds that when the author was putting forward or discussing an issue, the automatic assumption was 'this must be about boys'.

In personal terms, this was rather disconcerting. I had been a member of staff in the school for over fifteen years and yet the assumed link with a high-profile initiative seemed to have a clear impact on relationships, at least for a while. In sharing this reaction with the project's manager within the LEA, it became clear that he recognised it. He mentioned another colleague, also within one of the LEA's secondary schools, who was regarded as 'a national expert'. He had written and presented widely, on a key aspect of student behaviour within school, and yet was by-passed, even marginalised, by his own school's management when the issue was on the agenda. It was strangely comforting to know this and helped to dispel the feeling that it was something one individual had caused to happen within a single institution.

Rather ironically, however, this reaction on the part of my school helped the project to develop in a manner and direction that was to its ultimate benefit. Knowing that the mention of 'boys' would produce dropped heads and glazed eyes meant that debate had to be couched in broader terms, and attention given to introducing or modifying practices and processes which would have an impact on all students. Having to think in such terms was also a way of ensuring that whatever desirable change was introduced would be seen as an extension of existing good practice. There was the implication of it being manageable and sustainable, rather than an 'initiative' causing extra work and having a transient nature.

Whilst this was a message I attempted to convey to other local schools working in this area, it is, perhaps, too early to judge whether work has developed in this way. Additionally, at times, it seemed that the exposure of this issue in *The Times Educational Supplement*, did not support this message. For example, through May and June of 1997 debate teetered on the brink of an abyss where male writers would argue for the need to do something about boys, whilst female writers would point out the continuing need to 'do' something about girls. Such a debate seemed unhelpful in getting teachers to recognise that raising boys' achievement is one strand of a more general process of raising attainment, and, therefore, must involve all teachers and all students.

Issues arising from establishing a network of collaborating schools working with a seconded teacher

In establishing a national network of contacts with colleagues in secondary schools where work was being undertaken in raising boys' achievement, a recurring theme emerged. Teachers had little professional confidence in their sense that the ideas they had would be considered worthwhile outside the specific educational context in which they were generated. When specific practical projects were discussed, a typical response would be, 'We have tried this strategy, and evidence suggests it is having a positive impact; but it is very small-scale, almost common-sense really, and I don't know whether it would interest you.' Such comments often came from colleagues with many years of classroom experience, who were modifying their approaches to teaching and learning on the basis of reflection on that experience. Whilst many of the strategies could be regarded as small-scale, it is interesting to note that many of the strategies which were generated and applied involved challenging some of the most well-established and 'taken-for-granted' assumptions of classroom life.

As a corollary, one of the most positive and certainly unpredicted 'side effects' of work relating to the Raising Boys' Achievement project has been that it has reminded a significant number of teachers of several crucial points: that they are *major* players in determining which policies should be implemented to create improvement, how effective certain changes are proving to be in school, and how such change and improvement can be effectively sustained in a manageable way.

A second issue which emerged from working as a partially seconded teacher concerned the reaction of colleagues in my own school. For a significant period, it seemed as though most schools were interested in the work, apart from the one in which the author worked. Presentations were made to colleagues who looked vaguely uncomfortable, documents were produced which were judged to be interesting, but produced no action, and the idea that 'she has a bee in her bonnet about boys' was mentioned on more than one occasion. Whilst this was disconcerting at the time, although apparently also well recognised by other practitioner-researchers, it helped to shape an approach to work which was ultimately helpful. First, it had to be recognised that teachers were unlikely to change established practice in the classroom unless they felt emotionally committed to it and unless there was some quickly felt benefit – perhaps in terms of improved classroom relationships, better motivated students, or even personal professional satisfaction. Second, giving an immediate context for the work could develop initial interest and awareness. Rather than outlining the position nationally or even in the LEA, interest was generated when discussion of 'our' students took place. How are 'our' students getting on? What do 'our' students feel about their current experiences of teaching and learning? How can 'we' make improvements for 'our' students? In this way, the survey of student attitudes, 'How's It Going?', became as much an instrument of generating teacher enthusiasm for the project as for eliciting the views of boys and girls about their experiences of secondary schooling.

To produce a truly collaborating network, it was important that colleagues in individual schools should build up networks of contacts with each other, rather than operating through 'the middle', i.e. through the medium of the seconded teacher. This took longer to happen than had been envisaged. Termly collaborative meetings helped to establish the social aspects of the network as faces became familiar, and conversation would range broadly as colleagues established points of similarity and divergence between the current positions, agenda and development priorities for their schools. The project had progressed into its second year before there was evidence of colleagues from one of the participating schools contacting another directly to share information and develop ideas together. Interestingly, cross-pyramid work, linking feeder primary schools, or primary and middle schools, with the associated secondary school seemed to provide a clearer rationale for schools to work together. Was this because cross-pyramid collaborative working was seen to provide a natural way of ensuring coherence and progression for students? Or did cross-pyramid work represent a safer, less threatening milieu for debate, in the currently more competitive market situation in which schools find themselves? These questions must be left for the reader's consideration.

Summary

It is widely accepted that good teaching involves engaging students in their learning. Students must be motivated to participate, knowing that it is their contributions that will make a difference to effective learning. It is axiomatic to this work that effective school improvement strategies should be based on similar principles. The involvement and enthusiasm of teachers is central to the evolution, introduction, sustenance and evaluation of effective moves for improvement.

This chapter has discussed issues surrounding the creation of an enthusiastic, effective network of collaborating schools; a network with links 'outward' to the LEA and Higher Education and links 'inward' to the attitudes and aspirations of both teachers and students within school. Note has been made of the way in which teachers became the focus of generating strategies for improvement and how this was accomplished more within schools which were, in management terms, already established on a basis which welcomed contributions from all professional levels. Whilst teachers provided the main thrust for change, it was apparent that the very changes they advocated and implemented would modify their professional practice in ways which, initially, might feel uncomfortable. It was also apparent, however, that when teachers gained, or re-gained, confidence in their ability to initiate and evaluate change in the classroom, the benefits had a far broader influence than solely in the area of raising boys' achievement.

Acknowledgement

I wish to dedicate this chapter, with thanks and appreciation, to Dr Grant Roberts, who is my PhD supervisor at the University of Huddersfield.

References

Altrichter H (1993): *Teachers investigate their work*. London, Routledge.

Angus L (1993): The sociology of school effectiveness. *British Journal of Sociology of Education*. 14 (3), 333-345.

Arnold R (1995): *The improvement of schools through partnership: School, LEA and University*. Slough, NFER/EMIE.

Barber M (1996): *The learning game*. London, Gollancz.

Bell J (Ed) (1995) : *Teachers talk about teaching*. Buckingham, Open University Press.

Bennett N, Crawford M and Riches C (Eds) (1992): *Managing change in education*. London, PCP.

Bradford W A (1995): *The progress of boys in secondary school*. Unpublished MEd dissertation, University of Huddersfield.

Bradford W A (1996): *Raising Boys' Achievement: Secondary Version*. Huddersfield, Kirklees Education Advisory Service.

Brighouse T (1991): *What makes a good school?* Stafford, Network Educational Press.

Brown S and Mcintyre D (1993): *Making sense of teaching*. Buckingham, Open University Press.

Bush T (1986): *Theories of educational management*. London, Harper and Row.

Bush T (1988): *Action and theory in school management. E325, Block 1*. Buckingham, Open University Press.

Bush T and West-Burnham J (1994): *The principles of educational management*. Harlow, Longman.

Cooper P and McIntyre D C (1996): *Effective teaching and learning.* Buckingham: Open University Press.

Cullingford C (1993): Children's views on gender issues in school. *British Educational Research Journal*, 19 (5), 555-563.

Davies B (1990): *Education management for the 1990s.* London, Pitman.

De Gauna P R, Diaz G, Gonzalez V and Garaizar I (1995): Teachers' professional development as a process of critical action research. *Educational Action Research*, 3 (2), 183-194.

Downes P (1994): The gender effect. *Managing Schools Today*, 3 (5), 7-8.

EOC/OFSTED (1996): *The gender divide.* London, HMSO.

Fitzgibbon C T (1996): *Monitoring education: Indicators, quality and effectiveness.* London, Cassell.

Frith R and Mahony P (1994): *Promoting quality and equality in schools.* London, David Fulton.

Fullan M and Hargreaves A (1992): *What's worth fighting for in your school?* London, Cassell.

Haggarty L and Postlethwaite K (1995): Working as consultants on school-based teacher-identified problems. *Educational Action Research*, 3 (2), 169-181.

Hargreaves D H and Hopkins D (1991): *The empowered school.* London, Cassell.

Hargreaves D H and Hopkins D (1994): *Development planning for school improvement.* London, Cassell.

Hopkins D (1993): *A teacher's guide to classroom research.* Buckingham, Open University Press.

Hoyle E and John P D (1995): *Professional knowledge and professional practice.* London, Cassell.

Hutchinson B and Whitehouse P (1986): Action research, professional competence and school organisation. *British Educational Research Journal*, 12 (1), 85-94.

Keys W and Fernandes C (1993): *What do students think about school?* Slough, NFER.

Kincheloe J L (1991): *Teachers as researchers: qualitative inquiry as a path to empowerment.* London, Falmer Press.

Oliver P (Ed) (1996): *The management of educational change.* Hampshire, Arena.

Posch, P (1994): Changes in the culture of teaching and learning and implications for action research. *Educational Action Research*, 2 (2), 149-161.

Peters T J and Waterman R H (1982): *In search of excellence: lessons from America's best run companies.* New York, Harper and Row.

Reimer K M and Bruce B (1994): Building Teacher-Researcher Collaboration: dilemmas and strategies. *Educational Action Research*, 2 (4), 211-221.

Reynolds D and Cuttance P (Eds) (1992): *School effectiveness, research, policy and practice.* London: Cassell.

Ribbins P and Burridge E (Eds) (1994): *Improving education.* London, Cassell.

Riddell S and Brown S (Eds) (1991): *School effectiveness research: its messages for school improvement.* Edinburgh, HMSO.

Ruddock J, Chaplain R and Wallace G (Eds) (1996): *School improvement. What can pupils tell us?* London, David Fulton.

Scheerens J (1992): *Effective schooling.* London, Cassell.

Somekh B (1994): Inhabiting each other's castles: towards knowledge and mutual growth through collaboration. *Educational Action Research*, 2 (3), 357-381.

Somekh B (1995): The contribution of action research to development in social endeavours: a position paper on action research methodology. *British Educational Research Journal*, 21 (3), 339-355.

Strauss P (1995): No easy answers: the dilemmas and challenges of teacher research. *Educational Action Research*, 3 (1), 29-40.

Walker R (1985): *Doing research: a handbook for teachers.* London, Methuen.

West-Burnham J (1995): *Leadership and strategic management.* London, Pitman.

Wragg T (1997): Oh Boy! *The Times Educational Supplement* 2. 16/5/97, 4.

INDEX